ntents

1. INTRODU............ 6
2. MANAGIN............. 6
2.1 General F........ ... 7
2.2 Site Mana........ ... 8
2.3 Constructi..... ....ign and Management 2015............. 8
2.3.1 Introduction to CDM 2015................................ 8
2.3.2 Approach and Responsibilities 9
2.3.3 Structure of CDM 2015................................. 10

3. SAFE PLACES OF WORK.................................11
3.1 Access to the Workplace 11
3.1.1 General..11
3.1.2 Tidiness 12
3.2 Working at Height 12
3.2.1 Introduction to Work at Height Regulations 2005 12
3.2.2 Erection of Scaffolding................................ 15
3.2.3 Inspection of Scaffolding..............................17
3.2.4 Basic Checklist for Scaffold Inspection 18
3.2.5 Working on Scaffolds 20
3.2.6 Mobile Scaffold Tower 20
3.2.7 Trestle Scaffolding................................... 22
3.2.8 Working on Roofs 23
3.2.9 Fragile Roofs.. 25
3.2.10 Using Ladders Safely 26
3.3 Working Over Water 28
3.4 Excavations 29
3.5 Confined Spaces/Hazardous Atmospheres 30
3.6 Refurbishment Contracts.............................. 32
3.6.1 Unoccupied Premises 32
3.6.2 Occupied Premises................................... 33
3.7 Temporary Lighting 34
3.8 Protection from Excessive Noise 35

Contents

3.8.1	Hearing Protection.	35
3.9	Fire Precautions	36
3.9.1	Fire Extinguishers	37
4.	HAND TOOLS	39
4.1	Safe Storage	39
4.2	Electrically Operated Tools	39
4.3	Air Operated Tools and Equipment	41
4.4	Cartridge Assisted Tools	42
4.5	Power Saws.	43
4.5.1	Chain Saws.	44
4.5.2	Hand Held Circular Saws	45
4.6	Drills.	46
4.7	Breakers	46
4.8	Compactors.	46
4.9	Abrasive Wheels	47
4.9.1	Wheel Mounting.	47
4.9.2	Operating.	48
5.	WORKING WITH PLANT	49
5.1	Goods hoist.	49
5.2	Work Dumpers	50
5.3	Cranes and Lifting Equipment.	51
5.3.1	LOLER (Lifting Operations & Lifting Equipment Regulations)	51
5.3.2	Requirements for Banksmen	53
5.3.3	Working Near Cranes.	55
5.4	Working with Excavators.	55
5.5	Compressors	56
5.5.1	Starting Up.	57
5.5.2	Operating.	57
5.6	Rough Terrain Forklifts and Telescopic Handlers.	58
5.7	Woodworking Machinery.	60

Contents

5.8   Small Site Concrete/Mortar Mixers 62
5.9   Site Vehicles/Site Layout 63

6.   SPECIAL HAZARDS, RISKS AND SUBSTANCES 64
6.1   Demolition 64
6.2   Asbestos 65
6.3   Lead Paint 67
6.4   Dangerous and Hazardous Substances 68
6.4.1   Flammable Liquids 68
6.4.2   Liquefied Petroleum Gases 70
6.4.3   Substances Hazardous to Health 72

7.   WORKING NEAR EXISTING SERVICES 75
7.1   Electricity 75
7.1.1   Overhead Lines 75
7.1.2   Underground Cables 76
7.2   Gas, Water Mains and Sewers 78
7.2.1   Gas Mains 79
7.2.2   Water Mains 79
7.2.3   Sewers 80
7.3   Telecommunication Equipment 81

8.   OCCUPATIONAL HEALTH MANAGEMENT AND FIRST AID . . 82
8.1   Occupational Health Management - Introduction 82
8.1.1   Principles of Occupational Health Management 84
8.2   Occupational Health Risk Management System 85
8.2.1   Policy 85
8.2.2   Identify Health Risks 85
8.2.3   Eliminate Risk Where Possible 86
8.2.4   Identify Who is at Risk to the Residual Risks 86
8.2.5   Manage Residual Risks 86
8.2.6   Back to Work 87

Contents

8.3   Common Health Risks in Construction 87

8.3.1 Physical Ill Health Risks 87

8.3.2 Hazardous Substances 88

8.4   First Aid and Legal Requirements 90

8.4.1 First Aid Boxes, Qualified First Aiders and Appointed
Persons 90

8.4.2 First Aid Rooms 90

8.4.3 Stretchers and Supplementary Equipment 92

9.   WELFARE REQUIREMENTS 93

10.   PERSONAL PROTECTIVE EQUIPMENT (PPE) 94

10.1   Types of PPE 95

10.1.1 Hands 95

10.1.2 Eyes 95

10.1.3 Feet 96

10.1.4 Lungs 96

10.1.5 Ears 97

10.1.6 Backs 97

10.1.7 Safety Helmets 97

10.2   Protection Against the Operations of Others 98

10.2.1 Welding 99

10.2.2 Lasers 99

10.2.3 Site Radiography 100

11.   ACCIDENT REPORTING 101

12.   SAFETY SIGNS AND SIGNALS 102

12.1   Mandatory Signs 103

12.2   Warning Signs 104

12.3   Safety Signs 106

12.4   Fire Signs 107

Contents

12.5 Fire Extinguishers 108
12.6 Banksman Signals 109

13.   HOW TO GET MORE INFORMATION AND HELP 111
13.1 HSE Publications 111
13.2 HSE Contact 111
13.3 Guidance on CDM 112
13.4 Occupational Health & Safety Management 112

Introduction

1. INTRODUCTION

The law requires construction project team members to work together and create a safe and healthy workplace for those working on the project and the public who might be affected.

Most good practice is simply a matter of applying common sense and proper planning before starting an activity.

This booklet provides advice on managing health and safety on a construction project and where to go for further help and advice.

Contractors must assess and manage the risks arising from their work and the project Principal Contactor is required to manage the whole of the construction phase.

Supervisors can use the information and checklists in this booklet to guide their approach to planning and management of tasks on site.

Operatives will also find the booklet useful as guidance on what should be done to help create and maintain safe and healthy working conditions.

2. MANAGING HEALTH & SAFETY

The foundations for a healthy and safe site are:

- **People** – the right people with the necessary skills, knowledge and experience;

- **Planning** – careful planning during both design and construction phases including sound arrangements for cooperation and coordination between team members;

- **Plant and Equipment** – selection of suitable plant and equipment which is kept safe by proper maintenance and inspection arrangements; and

- **Positive Culture** – responsible working by everyone to generate a culture where people "Don't Walk By" unsafe conditions or behaviour.

There is a need to be aware of the requirements of health and safety legislation which is inevitably written in legal terms. However, easily understood information and guidance is freely available on the Health & Safety Executive (HSE) construction and general website pages and in other sources (see Section 13 of this booklet).

2.1   General Principles of Prevention

It is important to understand the general principles of prevention set out in the legislation which govern how businesses should consider and plan for safe and healthy working conditions. These are as follows:

- **Avoid risks** – where reasonably practicable by eliminating hazards e.g. ground level assembly avoids the risk of falling from height;

- **Substitute risks** – adopt non-dangerous or less dangerous working methods e.g. use water based paints rather than solvent based substances;

- **Evaluate risks** – which cannot be eliminated and combat those risks at source e.g. control dust with water suppression before relying on respiratory protective equipment (RPE);

- **Adapt work** – to the individual and to technical progress to reduce the effect of work on health;

- **Collective measures** – give priority to collective measures over individual protective measures e.g. install edge protection rather than use fall arrest system to prevent injury when falling from a roof; and

- **Instructions** – provide appropriate instructions to employees regarding the risks involved in the work and the precautions required.

2.2   Site Management

All project team members have responsibilities to prevent injury and ill-health. Contractors must consider potential hazards and risks when planning their work and adjust their methods, equipment and materials to ensure that everyone on site is considered.

It is important to remember that project Clients and Designers also have legal duties and contractors may need to discuss options to amend specification or design.

Specialist contractors and other contractors have great expertise in their activities and should be involved as soon as possible to secure the benefit of their knowledge.

The CDM Regulations 2015 require that project teams are established at a very early stage with arrangements in place for managing the project and developing co-operation in finding safe solutions for all significant hazards.

This preparatory design work is overseen by the client appointed Principal Designer who will plan, manage and monitor the pre-construction phase and coordinate health safety matters whilst design work is in progress (which will often overlap with the construction phase)

2.3   Construction Design and Management Regulations 2015

2.3.1 Introduction to CDM 2015

Aim

The Construction (Design and Management) Regulations 2015 (CDM 2015) set out the framework for managing risk during both the pre-construction and construction phases of a project.

Duties are placed on all project participants, including clients, designers and contractors.

The key aim is to focus attention on planning and management throughout the project from design concept onwards. Health and safety considerations are to be treated as an essential part of project development and not an afterthought or 'bolt on' extra.

2.3.2 Approach and Responsibilities

The effort devoted to planning and managing the project should be in proportion to the risks and complexity associated with the project. The focus should always be on the action necessary to eliminate, reduce and manage risks.

The documentation produced should help with communication and risk management. Any 'paperwork' which adds little to the management of risk is a waste of effort and can be a dangerous distraction from the real business or risk reduction and management.

The project team members with specific responsibilities under CDM 2015 are:

- **Client** – the main duty for the project client is to make sure their project is suitably managed throughout the life of the project and that a principal designer and principal contractor are appointed;

- **Principal Designer (PD)** – is appointed by the client to control the project pre-construction phase and plan, manage, monitor and coordinate health and safety during this phase when most design work is carried out;

- **Designers** – the definition of 'designers' includes architects, consulting engineers and quantity surveyors, or anyone who specifies and alters designs as part of their work. The main duty of design organisations is to (through their designs) eliminate, reduce or make it easier to control risks that may arise during the construction work, or in the use and maintenance of structures when used;

- **Principal Contractor (PC)** – is appointed by the client to manage the construction phase and plan, manage, monitor and coordinate health and safety during this phase when all construction work takes place. Workers must be consulted by the PC in good time on matters which may affect their health, safety or welfare;

- **Contractors** – are sole traders or businesses in charge of carrying out construction work (e.g. building, altering, maintaining or demolishing). The main duty of contractors is to plan, manage and monitor the work under their control in a way that ensures the health and safety of anyone it might affect (including members of the public); and

- **Workers** – all individual workers who carry out the work e.g. plumbers, electricians, scaffolders, painters, decorators, steel erectors and labourers, as well as supervisors e.g. foremen and charge hands. Worker duties include cooperating with their employer and others, reporting anything they see which might endanger the health and safety of themselves or others.

2.3.3 Structure of CDM 2015

The CDM Regulations 2015 are set out as follows:

Part 1 – Introduction – application and interpretation of terms used in the regulations;

Part 2 – Client duties – project management arrangements required, providing pre-construction information, appointing project principals. The client is also responsible for notifying projects to HSE;

Part 3 – Health and safety duties and roles – sets out general duties and those of designers, principal designers, principal contractors and contractors. This Part contains the requirements for a construction phase plan, health and safety file and consultation with the workforce;

Part 4 – General requirements for all construction sites – this Part explains the precautions required for particular hazards found on construction projects e.g. site access, tidiness, demolition, excavations, structural stability and fire etc.

CDM 2015 is in **addition** to other regulations covering, for example:

- Work at Height
- Asbestos
- Lead and Hazardous / Dangerous substances
- Noise and vibration
- Manual handling
- Work equipment
- Lifting operations
- Confined space working

3. SAFE PLACES OF WORK

3.1 Access to the Workplace

3.1.1 General

A significant proportion of injuries are caused during simple movement of people to and from workplaces on site. It is therefore vital that proper access from place to place is created and kept safe to avoid such accidents.

This objective can be supported by checking the following:

- **Access** – is provided to reach each workplace e.g. good roadways separated from pedestrian routes, gangways, hoists, staircases, ladders and scaffolding;

- **Walkways** – are level (as far as is reasonably practicable) and free from obstruction;

- **Edge protection** – is in place to prevent falls of people and materials;

- **Openings** – in floors are covered with securely fixed covers or fenced;

- **Lighting** – artificial lighting is available when required;

- **Materials** – are stored in safe positions and the site kept tidy;
- **Waste** – arrangements are in place for the gathering and disposal of scrap; and
- **Projections** – e.g. nails in timber hammered flat or removed completely.

3.1.2 Tidiness

A tidy site is a safe site. Many accidents are caused by people tripping, slipping and falling over materials and equipment.

Everyone can make a significant contribution to safety, merely by applying common sense practice which includes:

- **Tidy up** – as you go and do not leave rubbish lying about;
- **Obstructions** – keep gangways, aisles or stairways clear of tools or materials;
- **Clean up** – spilled oil, grease or liquids without delay; and
- **Waste** – deposit waste and refuse in agreed safe positions.

3.2   Working at height

3.2.1 Introduction to the Working at Height Regulations 2005

Falls from height account for the greatest number of serious and fatal injuries in the construction industry although there are many simple and cost effective preventive solutions now available.

The Work at Height Regulations 2005 sets out the legal duties relating to work at height across all industry sectors. The regulations require duty holders to ensure:

- Proper planning and organisation of all work at height.
- Competent and supervised workforce including trainees

- Assessment of the risks from work at height and selection/use of appropriate work equipment
- Fragile surface risks strictly managed e.g. danger from falling through fragile rooflights etc. must be properly controlled.
- Inspection and maintenance of all equipment for work at height

Remember: Work at height can include working at ground level e.g. next to an excavation.

The objective is to make sure work at height is properly planned, supervised and carried out in a safe manner. The approaches you can adopt for work at height are to:

- **Avoid work at height** where it reasonably practicable to do so, e.g. by assembly at ground level and:
- **Prevent any person falling** a distance liable to cause personal injury e.g. by using a scaffold platform with double guard-rail and toe boards; and
- **Arrest a fall** with equipment to minimise the distance and consequences of a fall, e.g. safety nets, where work at height cannot be avoided or the fall prevented.

The Principles of Prevention apply and The Hierarchy of Control Measures is on the following page.

Safe Places of Work

The Hierarchy of Control Measures with Practical Examples

Hierarchy	Examples
AVOID	Design out the need to work at height. Cast in mesh in riser ducts in floor slabs at position of services. Erect handrails/edge protection at ground level and crane in. Fix nets by working from the floor below using extending poles.
PREVENT by using an existing place of work PREVENT by using work equipment COLLECTIVE	A flat roof with a permanent edge protection. A tanker roof with a fixed edge protection. Access equipment fitted with guardrails: MEWPs, scissor lifts, mast climbers, cradles, tower scaffolds, and independent scaffolds.
PREVENT by using work equipment PERSONAL	PPE used in a way so it is impossible to get to a fall position, e.g. work restraint.
MITIGATE by using work equipment to minimise distance and consequences COLLECTIVE	Nets and soft landing systems, such as air bags positioned close under work surface.
MITIGATE by using work equipment to minimise distance and consequences PERSONAL	A personal fall-arrest system with the anchorage point sited above the head (fall factor zero). Rope access. A work positioning system. A personal fall arrest system with anchorage level at sternum/dorsal attachment point (fall factor 1).
MITIGATE using work equipment to minimise the consequences PERSONAL	A personal injury system (life jacket whilst working next to unguarded water)
MITIGATE through training and instruction or other means	Ladders; hop ups; silts.

3.2.2   Erection of Scaffolding

Falls from scaffolding account for a significant proportion of deaths and injuries. In addition, the collapse of a scaffold holds the potential for a major catastrophic event.

Scaffolders must be competent for the type of scaffolding work they are undertaking and should have received appropriate training relevant to the type and complexity of scaffolding on which they are working.

Appropriate levels of supervision must also be provided taking into account the complexity of the work and the levels of training and competence of the scaffolders involved.

As a minimum requirement, every scaffold team should contain a competent scaffolder who has received training for the type and complexity of the scaffold to be erected, altered or dismantled.

Trainee scaffolders must work under the direct supervision of a trained and competent scaffolder. Operatives are classed as 'trainees' until they have completed the approved training and assessed as competent.

Erection, alteration and dismantling of all scaffolding structures (basic or complex) should be done under the direct supervision of a competent person. For complex structures this would usually be an 'Advanced Scaffolder' or an individual who has received training in a specific type of system scaffold for the complexity of the configuration involved.

Scaffolding operatives should be up to date with the latest changes to safety guidance and good working practices within the scaffolding industry. Giving operatives job specific pre-start briefings and regular toolbox talks is a good way of keeping them informed.

Guidance on the relevant expertise of Scaffolders and Advanced scaffolders including details of which structures they are deemed competent to erect can be obtained from the Construction Industry Scaffolders Record Scheme (CISRS) website.

The following list highlights some key points to check when scaffolding is used:

- **materials** for the job sufficient, inspected and in good working condition.
- **timber sole plates** are of adequate dimensions to provide safe bearing.
- **metal base plates** are used under all standards.
- **joints between tubes** are staggered vertically and horizontally.
- **correct type of couplers** are used for all connections.
- **scaffold boards** are in good condition.
- **standards** are upright and set out in accordance with the drawings or sketches provided.
- **ledger bracing** provided with alternative pairs of standards to the full height of the scaffolding. Exceptions may be made for the bottom and top lifts where access is required.
- **façade bracing** is fitted to the full height of the scaffold.
- **scaffold tied** securely to the structure.
- **working platforms** are fully boarded.
- **edge protection** is installed comprising double guard rails and a toe board.

In addition, it is important to adhere to the following safety rules:

- **Incomplete scaffold** provided with blocked access or a notice indicating that the scaffold is not to be used.
- **Correct spanners** used to ensure fittings are correctly tightened.
- **Dismantling operations** undertaken in proper sequence of work so that the scaffold is secure at each stage.
- **Lower materials etc.** safely e.g. do not throw or drop materials.
- **Lifts or fans** must not be used to store materials as dismantling proceeds.

3.2.3 Inspection of Scaffolding

It is the responsibility of the scaffold user/hirer to ensure that all scaffolding has been inspected as follows:

- following installation/before first use.
- at an interval of no more than every 7 days thereafter.
- following any circumstances liable to jeopardise the safety of the installation e.g. high winds.

All scaffolding inspection should be carried out by a competent person whose combination of knowledge, training and experience is appropriate for the type and complexity of the scaffold. Competence may have been assessed under the CISRS or an individual may have received training in inspecting a specific type of system scaffold from a manufacturer/supplier.

A non-scaffolder who has attended a scaffold inspection course (e.g. a site manager) could be deemed competent to inspect a basic scaffold structure.

The scaffold inspection report should note any defects or matters which could give rise to a risk to health and safety and any corrective actions taken. The record should be made even when corrective actions are taken promptly. This record will assist with the identification of any recurring problem.

In order to have a systematic and effective method of inspection a standard form or checklist should be produced which is specific to the scaffold being inspected. The CIP Record Book ROIF911 can be used.

Special attention should be given to ground conditions and the effectiveness of baseplates after rain or thawing of frozen ground. Particular attention should be given to sheeted scaffolding, during and after any significant winds. People inspecting sheeted scaffolds must understand how the scaffold has been designed.

3.2.4 Basic Checklist for Scaffold Inspection (Tubes & Fittings)

Description	Inspection	Action
Foundations	Walk round the scaffold and check for: subsidence of the ground, cavities underneath soleplates dislocation of base plates.	Rectify with adjustable base plates. Fill with concrete. Restore in place.
Standards	Stand back in front of each standard and check for: plumbness, any signs of buckling in first 3-4 lifts.	Stop using scaffold in the affected section until made good.
Horizontal Lacing	Check in first 3-4 lifts if the position of ledgers and transoms. First lift is of extreme importance, and the standards must be effectively braced in both directions at ground level. Vertical distance between horizontal bracing in the first lift must not be greater than in subsequent lifts.	Replace any missing bracing.
Diagonal Bracing	Transverse bracing to alternative pairs of standards may be fixed either to ledgers or directly to standards. Façade bracing to be fixed to transoms with right angle couplers and extended from the ground level.	As above.
a) Standards b) Ledgers c) Transoms d) Diagonal Bracing e) Scaffold Ties	Make sure that the members (standard ledgers, transoms and diagonal bracing) are not supporting any other loading, vertical or horizontal, coming from external structures like cranes, hoists, loading towers, rubbish chutes, etc. These structures should be designed as independent load carriers with separate ties to the building.	
a) Weather Protection b) Safety Nets and Fans	When (a) and (b) are incorporated in the scaffold detailed relevant drawings should be available from the sub-contractor for checking purposes.	
Ladders	Every ladder must stand on a firm and even base and be supported only by the stiles. The ladder must be securely held in position at top and bottom by fixings to the stiles. The ladder should project at least 1m above the landing platform. Inspect all rungs for soundness.	

Description	Inspection	Action
Extended Scaffold Skeleton	Make sure that vertical and horizontal joints in tubes are staggered. Not more than one lift can be erected above the scaffold ties.	
Mixed Construction of Steel and Alloy Scaffold	No mixing is permitted of steel and alloy scaffold components of the same designation. All standards must be made either in steel or alloy. Similar requirements apply to ledgers, transoms, bracing and ties. Handrails must be made of the same material as ledgers.	The final arrangement to be checked by a competent engineer.
Scaffold Ties	Check ties in first 3-4 lifts. Each tie must be fixed to both ledgers as near to standards as possible. Horizontal spacing must not exceed three bays. Vertical spacing at each story height starting from the first floor or at every other lift.	Replace any missing tie.
Scaffold	Check the position and fixing of all scaffold ties.	As above.
Decking	1. The working platform should be at least 600mm wide and closely boarded, each board having at least 3 supports. 2. Boards should be butted and they should over sail their last support by at least 50mm but not more than 150mm. Lapping is permissible if bevel pieces provided to prevent tripping. 3. Precautions should be taken to hold down decking in high winds. 4. The space between the edge of the platform and the face for the building must be as small as possible. Where people need to sit on the platform edge to work, the space should not exceed 300mm.	Do not use scaffold until 1, 2 and 4 are rectified. 3 Nail steel straps to hold boards together.
Guard Rails & Toeboards	1. Both guard rails and toe boards should be fixed to the inside of the standards and remain in position before decking is removed. 2. The main guard rail should be at not less than 950mm above the decking. 3. Toe boards should be at least 150mm high above the decking and the clear spacing between the guard rails and toe boards should not exceed 470mm. Stacked material needs special attention.	The decking must not be used until conditions 1, 2 and 3 are complied with.

3.2.5 Working on Scaffolds

When working on scaffolds you should follow the simple general rules below:

- **Modifications** – never remove or interfere with the scaffolding especially ties, guard rails, toe boards and ladders. Alterations to scaffolding must be made by authorised persons.

- **Incomplete** – only use a scaffold when it is complete and not during erection, dismantling or when the scaffold is in any way incomplete.

- **Defects** – report to the supervisor any scaffolding which appears defective.

- **Stacking** – leave a gangway at least two boards wide for access when stacking materials on a scaffold. Stack materials so that they cannot be accidentally knocked off the platform and use brick guards or other suitable protection if necessary.

- **Safe Load** – before loading materials on to a scaffold check the safe load capacity of the working platform. Load materials as near to standards as possible.

- **Tools and materials** – do not leave lying about on working platforms. Materials should always be lowered from height by suitable tackle or disposed of through a properly constructed chute and NOT thrown or tipped.

- **Access** – use access ladders and stairs provided and never climb up or down the scaffolding.

3.2.6 Mobile Scaffold Towers

Tower scaffolds are one way to work safely at height. However, many people are injured each year when they fall from towers or when the tower overturns.

The type of tower selected must be suitable for the work and erected and dismantled by people who have been trained and are competent to do so. There are a number of organisations that provide training for the safe erection and use of tower scaffolds.

The incidents which occur are mainly caused by:

- **Dangerous methods of erection or dismantling** – where a safe system is not being followed;

- **Defects in the erected scaffold** – where the tower structure is incorrectly assembled or a platform guardrail is missing;

- **Misuse of the scaffold** – where a ladder is used on a tower causing it to overturn or when a person falls while the tower is being moved.

Those using tower scaffolds should also be trained in the potential dangers and precautions required during use. Tower scaffold provision and use must be properly managed and include rigorous scaffold inspection arrangements.

In order to use a mobile tower in safety it is important to follow certain basic rules.

- **Safety instructions** – always obtain and follow the supplier instructions regarding safe erection and use of the particular tower.

- **Competence** – a mobile scaffold must be erected by persons competent to do so.

- **Maximum height** – for outside use, the maximum tower height should not be more three times the minimum width (e.g. a tower with a height of 15m should have a base width of 5m) and 3.5 times for inside use. If these height-to-base ratios have to be exceed, properly designed outriggers must be used or the scaffold tied to a stable structure.

- **Edge protection** – guard rails and toe boards must be fitted.

- **Stability** – towers must only be used on firm level ground.

- **Locking** – wheel locks must be active before climbing a tower.

- **Moving** – the movement of a tower should be carried out by pushing at the base and never when a person or materials are on the platform.
- **Obstructions** – keep the tower well clear of electrical cables and equipment when moving a tower and pay careful attention to any other possible obstruction at the base or overhead.
- **Defects** – a tower which appears defective should be reported at once and an "Incomplete scaffold" or a "Do not use" sign put in place.
- **Step ups** – working from boxes or steps on top of the tower to increase the height must never be attempted.
- **Authorisation** – towers belonging to others should not be used without authorisation.
- **Access** – adequate means of access to the working platform should be provided by means of a ladder within the tower.
- **Loading** – the safe working load recommended by the tower manfacturer should never be exceeded.

3.2.7 Trestle Scaffolds

Trestle scaffolds are simple working platforms supported on "A" frames or similar folding supports such as painters' trestles or pairs of steps. Use only where there is low risk of a person falling from the platform and only for light work of short duration.

For working over longer periods a more substantial scaffold should be erected.

Trestles should be examined before use and rejected if:

- cross bearers are loose or damaged.
- hinges are broken or damaged or screws are missing.
- stiles are defective.

One third of the height of a trestle should be above the working platform.

Lightweight staging should be used to form the platform which must be at least 600mm wide. Trestle scaffolds must be provided with an independent means of access to the platform e.g. step ladder.

3.2.8 Working on Roofs

Work on roofs involves a high risk of injury unless proper procedures are followed and precautions taken. Everyone involved in managing or carrying out work on roofs should be aware of the following facts:

- **High risk** – almost one in five deaths in construction work involves roof work. Some are specialist roofers, but many are just repairing and cleaning roofs.

- **Main causes** – the main causes of death and injury are falling from roof edges or openings, through fragile roofs and through fragile rooflights.

- **Equipment and people** – many accidents could be avoided if the most suitable equipment was used and those undertaking the work were given adequate information, instruction, training and supervision.

All work on roofs is highly dangerous, even if a job only takes a few minutes. Proper precautions are needed to control the risk. Those carrying out the work must be trained, competent and instructed in use of the precautions required.

A 'method statement' is the common way to help manage work on roofs and communicate the precautions to those involved.

On business premises contractors should work closely with the client and agree arrangements for managing the work.

Safe Places of Work

Before working on any type of roof you should know and follow the basic rules set out below:

- **Assess the risk** – contractors must assess the risks; decide on the precautions required; record the significant findings; and review the assessment as necessary. Do not overcomplicate the process. For many firms your work at height risks will be well known and the necessary control measures easy to apply.

- **Means of access** – make sure that a means of access to the roof is available and that it is safe and sufficient to use.

- **Collective Protection** – in almost every case, guard rails and toe boards must be provided along the roof edge, securely fixed in position and of adequate strength. If these measures are not implemented, alternative safe methods of working must be identified and put in place.

- **Crawling ladders etc.** – for work on a sloping roof (a pitch of more than 10%) crawling ladders or crawling boards should be provided.

- **Fall arrest systems** – there may be circumstances where the assessment shows that use of a fall arrest system is the only safe way of working. This equipment must be used in the conditions specified by a safe system of work. Collective measures such as nets and soft landing systems should be used in preference to equipment which will provide individual protection (e.g. a safety harness).

- **Openings** – in the roof must be securely covered or suitably protected by guard rails and toe boards. Covers should either be securely fixed in position or clearly marked to indicate the purpose e.g. "Do not remove this cover - hole below". In many cases, giving thought at the design stage may eliminate or mitigate the risk e.g. casting in protection at the same time as forming the opening.

3.2.9 Fragile Roofs

Falls through fragile roof surfaces are a major cause of death and life-changing injuries. These surfaces and materials will not safely support the weight of a person and any materials they may be carrying.

All roofs should be treated as fragile until a competent person has confirmed that they are non-fragile. In particular, the following types of roof materials are likely to be fragile:

- **Fibre-cement sheets** – non-reinforced sheets irrespective of profile type;
- **Rooflights** – particularly those in the roof plane that can be difficult to see in certain light conditions or when hidden by paint;
- **Liner panels** – on built-up sheeted roofs;
- **Metal sheets** – where corroded;
- **Glass** – including wired glass;
- **Chipboard** – or similar material where rotted; and
- **Others** – including wood wool slabs, slates and tiles.

All these material have been involved in fatal or serious falls. Before working on or near this type of roof material you must take full account of the type and condition of the material and put appropriate safety precautions in place.

Effective precautions are required for all work on or near fragile surfaces, no matter how short the duration, whether the work concerns construction, maintenance, repair, cleaning or demolition.

The HSE website contains detailed free guidance on the dangers presented by fragile surfaces and the precautions required. This guidance should be consulted by all involved in such work.

Key precautions required are:

- **Avoidance** – plan and organise work to keep people away from fragile surfaces so far as possible, e.g. by working from below the surface on a mobile elevating work platform or other suitable platform.

- **Control** – work on or near fragile surfaces requires a combination of stagings, guard rails, fall restraint, fall arrest and safety nets slung beneath and close to the roof.

- **Communication** – warning notices must be fixed on the approach to any fragile surface. Those carrying out the work must be trained, competent and instructed in use of the precautions required.

- **Co-operation** – on business premises, contractors should work closely with the client and agree arrangements for managing the work.

3.2.10 Using ladders safely

A pre-use check should be carried out every time before a ladder is used to make sure that it is safe for use.

A pre-use check should be carried out by the user before using the ladder for a work task and after something has changed, i.e. a ladder dropped or moved from a dirty area to a clean area (check state or condition of feet).

The benefit of conducting pre-use checks is that they provide the opportunity to spot any immediate serious defects before they cause an injury.

When using a leaning ladder to carry out a task take the following basic precautions:

- **Carrying** – only carry light materials and tools. Read the manufacturer labels on the ladder and assess the risks;

- **Overreaching** – do not overreach. Make sure your belt buckle (navel) stays within the stiles;

- **Length** – make sure the ladder is long enough and high enough for the task;

- **Loading** – do not overload a ladder including the user weight and the equipment or materials carried;

- **Angle** – make sure the ladder angle is at 75°. The 1 in 4 rule can be used i.e. 1 unit out for every 4 units up;

- **Grip** – always grip a ladder and face the ladder rungs while climbing or descending. Do not slide down the stiles;

- **Moving** – do not move or extend ladders whilst standing on the rungs;

- **Position** – do not work from the top three rungs of the ladder and ensure the ladder extends at least 1 m (three rungs) above the working position;

- **Ground** – do not stand ladders on moveable objects e.g. pallets, bricks, lift trucks, tower scaffolds, excavator buckets, vans, or mobile elevating work platforms;

- **Powerlines** – do not work within 6 m horizontally of any overhead power line, unless the line has been made dead or it is protected with insulation. Use a non-conductive ladder (e.g. fibreglass or timber) for any electrical work;

- **Climbing** – maintain three points of contact when climbing (this means a hand and two feet) and wherever possible at the work position. Where you cannot maintain a handhold, other than for a brief period (e.g. to hold a nail while starting to knock it in, starting a screw etc), other measures should be taken to prevent a fall or reduce the consequences of a fall; and

- **Secure** – a leaning ladder should be secured e.g. by tying the ladder to prevent it from slipping either outwards or sideways. A strong upper resting point should be used. Do not rest a ladder against weak upper surfaces e.g. glazing or plastic gutters. An effective stability device can also be used.

3.3 Working Over Water

Falling into the water and drowning is an ever-present danger when working over or adjacent to water.

The following precautions should always be followed:

- **Tripping** – make sure working platforms are secure and free from tripping hazards (tools, wire, timber, etc.). Slippery surfaces should be treated immediately;

- **Workplace** – check that guard rails and toe boards are firmly fixed in position and access ladders secured to prevent movement;

- **Life jacket** – wear a life jacket which is properly fastened. Check that there are no punctures and that inflation devices (where fitted) are effective;

- **Safety nets etc.** – when required, use the safety nets or safety harness provided;

- **Lifebuoys** – check that lifebuoys or throw-bags fitted with lines are available for use;

- **Safety boat** – where available ensure the boat is manned and that any motor boat is fuelled and ready to be used;

- **Alarm and rescue** – know the routine for raising the alarm and the rescue drill;

- **Lone working** – do not work alone over water; and

- **Safety box** – ensure the safety box is available with contents including suitable measures to help hypothermia (e.g. foil blankets).

3.4 Excavations

Every year people die or are seriously injured by the collapse or falling materials whilst working in excavations. The main risks are from:

- **Excavations collapsing** – and burying or injuring people working in the excavation;
- **Materials falling** – over the sides and into the excavation; and
- **People or plant** – falling into excavations.

Remember: ***No ground can be relied upon to stand unsupported in all circumstances.*** Depending on conditions, a cubic metre of soil can weigh in excess of 1.5 tonnes.

Trenchless techniques should always be considered at the design stage as they replace the need for major excavations.

Underground and overhead services may also present a fire, explosion, electrical or other hazard which will need to be assessed and managed

Follow the guidelines below to achieve and maintain a safe working place:

- **Temporary support** – before digging any trench, pit, tunnel, or other excavations, decide what temporary support will be required and plan the precautions to be taken. Make sure the equipment and precautions needed (trench sheets, props, baulks etc.) are available on site **before** work starts.

- **Battering excavation sides** – battering the excavation sides to a safe angle of repose may also make the excavation safer. In granular soils, the angle of slope should be less than the natural angle of repose of the material being excavated. In wet ground a considerably flatter slope will be required.

- **Loose materials** – may fall from spoil heaps into the excavation. Edge protection should include toe boards or other means e.g. projecting trench sheets or box sides to protect against falling materials. Head protection should be worn.

Safe Places of Work

- **Undermining structures** – check that excavations do not undermine scaffold footings, buried services or the foundations of nearby buildings or walls. Decide if extra support for the structure is needed before you start. Surveys of the foundations and the advice of a structural engineer may be required.

- **Plant and vehicles** – do not park plant and vehicles close to the sides of excavations. The extra loadings can make the sides of excavations more likely to collapse.

- **People falling** – edges of excavations should be protected with substantial barriers where people are liable to fall into them. To achieve this use: guard rails and toe boards inserted into the ground immediately next to the supported excavation side; or fabricated guard rail assemblies that connect to the sides of the trench box the support system itself e.g. using trench box extensions or trench sheets longer than the trench depth.

- **Inspection** – a competent person who fully understands the dangers and necessary precautions should inspect the excavation at the start of each shift. Excavations should also be inspected after any event that may have affected their strength or stability, or after a fall of rock or earth. A record of the inspections will be required and any faults that are found should be corrected immediately.

3.5 Confined Spaces and Hazardous Atmospheres

Fatal and serious accidents are caused by persons entering live foul sewers, manholes, bored piles, trenches, tanks etc. without the necessary tests being carried out or the correct work equipment and safety rescue equipment being provided.

Work should only be carried out in a confined space when there are no alternative ways of undertaking the work without entering the space.

Dangerous atmospheres can arise where there is a lack of oxygen or when toxic or flammable gases are present. These may be due to exhaust gases from plant and transport, chemical reactions in the ground, decomposition of sludge in a sewer, leaks from gas mains, or the presence of petrol and various kinds of waste from factories and trade premises, welding operations and so on.

Many of these accidents would have been avoided if supervisory staff and operatives had been properly trained and the work carried out on a 'Permit to work' system.

Persons engaged in such operations must be physically and mentally suitable and properly trained for the job.

The following check list is a reminder of the main precautions required:

- **System of work** – do not enter or leave a confined space (trench, manhole, tank, bored pile, foul sewer) otherwise than in accordance with a system of work set out by the employer and with specific instruction from the supervisor.

- **Monitoring atmosphere** – equipment for monitoring the atmosphere must be provided and used by a competent person. You must not enter the confined space until the competent person is satisfied that entry is safe. Monitoring must continue whilst operatives are working inside. Persons must leave immediately if told to do so.

- **Inflowing liquids etc.** – asphyxiation or drowning can occur if persons are trapped by an unexpected influx of liquid or free-flowing solid. Any valves, gateways or hoppers that could release liquids or solids should be locked off at all times.

- **Ventilation** – adequate fresh air ventilation must be provided in appropriate circumstances.

- **Rescue equipment etc.** – check that all necessary safety and rescue equipment is available on site at the actual work location.

- **Incident assistance** – it is essential that no less than two persons work on a confined spaces operation and that incident assistance is readily available and methods to call-up help are agreed. Assistance must be readily available at all times.

- **Openings and holes** – when working at a manhole in the road or public area guard stands must be provided and the appropriate traffic signs displayed.

- **Emergencies** – everyone must clearly understand what is required in the event of an emergency.

- **Training** – make sure persons have been trained in the use of the safety and rescue equipment.

3.6   Refurbishment Works

Refurbishing existing properties gives rise to distinctive health and safety problems. In some cases the situation is made more difficult by the property remaining occupied whilst refurbishing is carried out.

Follow these basic rules to secure the safety of operatives and others:

3.6.1   Unoccupied Premises

- **Services** – before starting any activity check that public utility services e.g. gas, electricity, water etc. have been disconnected.

- **Stability** – much refurbishing work involves a degree of demolition and rebuilding of the structure. Never assume that the basic structure is sound and do not attempt any kind of demolition unless instructed by a competent person.

- **Asbestos** – highly dangerous asbestos containing materials (ACMs) are often found in areas which might not appear to present a risk e.g. soffits, ceiling tiles, room partitions, fire protection on steelwork, insulation in plant rooms etc. An asbestos refurbishment / demolition survey is required before refurbishment work starts in order to identify any ACMs present and to determine the correct precautions required.

- **Temporary works** – it will frequently be necessary to provide temporary support and shoring to the structure when demolition and replacement is necessary. These works must be carried out in accordance with the drawings or sketches provided and under the supervision of an experienced and competent person.

- **Materials** – demolition materials should be removed immediately from the building through properly devised rubbish chutes or similar means. These materials must never be allowed to accumulate on floors, landings or balconies which may become grossly overloaded and collapse.

- **Unknown conditions** – decayed or rotting timber may require removal. Proceed with caution as material where persons are standing may be rotten and liable to fail. Brickwork is frequently suspect in old buildings. Do not tie scaffolding to brickwork unless it has been established by a competent person as being in good condition.

- **Fire** – check that adequate fire extinguisher facilities are readily available. The fire hazard is considerable in during refurbishment projects.

- **Lighting** – make sure that adequate lighting is installed especially in stair wells.

3.6.2 Occupied Premises

When working in occupied premises, the health and safety of the occupants must also be considered.

In addition to all the above points the following should be observed:

- Means of escape – fire escape routes access ways from occupied areas must be kept clear and unblocked at all times.

Safe Places of Work

- **Substances etc.** – toxic or dangerous materials or sharp tools must be secure and not left unattended in places where children have access.

- **Openings etc.** – warn the occupants and fence off the area where floorboards are removed and replace the boards as soon as possible. At the end of the day do not leave work areas unguarded at if likely to be a danger for a tenant e.g. holes in floors, missing staircase hand rails etc.

- **Electricity** – on housing projects services may remain connected for the convenience of occupants. Services should be disconnected whilst work is carried out whenever necessary to prevent danger. It may be necessary to re-connect when work finishes for the day. Beware of live electrical terminals temporarily uncovered. An electrician should check that live electrical conductors are adequately protected.

- **Ladders** – do not leave ladders where children might use to gain access to scaffolds or other dangerous areas.

- **Respect** – treat occupants and their homes with respect at all times. Clear up as work progresses and take particular care when working near schools or other areas where children are present.

3.7   Temporary Lighting

Adequate lighting (either natural or artificial) is essential to site safety. It is also important that any temporary electrical installations are installed by qualified electricians with equipment and voltage (110V) suitable for safe use in the temporary environment.

If temporary lighting is provided in the workplace follow the rules below for safe use.

- **Interference** – do not interfere with the installation in any way.

- **Portable lamps** – when using portable inspection lamps do not drag the cable over the ground or round corners. This could damage the insulation and make equipment unsafe.

- **Extension cables** – where extension cables are in use splash-proof plugs and sockets should be fitted.

- **Wet conditions** – do not let trailing cables or connections come into contact with wet or damp conditions.

- **Back up** – consider emergency lighting systems with back-up power source in the event of a power failure.

3.8 Protection from Excessive Noise

Noise from plant, processes and power tools can cause, over a period of time, progressive and irreversible loss of hearing. Ringing or rushing noise in the ears can also occur (known as tinnitus).

Hearing loss makes communication difficult which may lead to accidents when instructions are not being heard or misheard.

Deafness caused by excessive noise at work develops very gradually and cannot be repaired once the damage has been done.

Precautions are required to protect hearing including the following basic rules:

3.8.1 Hearing Protection

- **One Metre Rule** – if it is necessary to shout to be heard by someone 1m away, it is likely that there is a noise problem requiring action.

- **Assessment** – where there is a potential risk noise exposure must be assessed to establish the degree of risk and decide if control measures and hearing protection is required.

- **Hearing protection (HP)** – where hearing protection is assessed as required it should be worn at all times. All forms of hearing protection must be fit properly and be treated with care.
- **Selection of HP** – different types / frequencies of noise require the use of appropriate types of hearing protectors. Check that the protection supplied is suitable.
- **Inspection** – the condition of hearing protectors should be checked regularly to see they are in good condition. The hands of users must be clean before using HP inserted in the user's ear.

3.9   Fire Precautions

Fires on construction sites most frequently involve the following types of 'fuel':

- Compressed gases – e.g. propane and acetylene
- Flammable liquids – including many types of adhesive; and
- Waste material – e.g., wood shavings and cellular plastics materials.

In addition to fuel a fire requires, oxygen and a source of ignition. Consideration of these three factors is crucial to managing all fire risks.

Everyone on site should be aware of the fire risk, know the precautions to prevent a fire and the action to be taken if fire does break out.

Always keep in mind the following basic rules.

- **Fighting fires** – know where firefighting appliances are located and the correct type of extinguisher for specific types of fire (see the following page).
- **Raise the alarm** – if fire breaks out arrange for someone to call the fire brigade. Do not continue trying to fight the blaze if large quantities of fumes are being emitted in a closed space. Leave the building and ensure an alarm is given to stop people entering into danger.

- **Drying clothes** – many fires are caused when drying wet clothes. Heaters for this purpose, gas, oil or electric, should be mounted on and backed with non-flammable material, enclosed in a stout wire mesh with effective air space to prevent clothing being placed directly upon the heater. Radiator type heating units are preferred to eliminate sources of ignition.

- **Ignition sources** – check that all lights and heaters are extinguished at the end of each working day. When 'hot work' has finished make sure that the workplace is examined an hour after work has finished for signs of combustion.

- **Waste control** – keep work areas clean and tidy and do not allow rubbish or other waste to accumulate.

- **Hot work** – if you use blow lamps or similar equipment make sure that there is no fire risk to adjacent materials. Wooden floors and other combustible materials must be covered with sand or other non-combustible material.

- **Permits to work** – all hot work should be carried out under a permit to work (PTW) with firefighting equipment adjacent to the work.

- **Means of escape** – escape routes should be planned, clearly identified and kept free from obstruction.

- **Fire alarm** – the fire risk assessment may have identified the need for a comprehensive fire alarm system. Make sure you are aware of the location of activation points.

3.9.1 Fire Extinguishers

Extinguishers are colour coded to denote types of fires that can be extinguished. Most extinguishers are red and have bands or colour coded zones on the cylinder to denote use. Some older extinguishers are painted entirely in the colour denoting use.

Safe Places of Work

Extinguisher type	Action and suitability
Water Colour: Red	Cooling. For fires in ordinary combustible building materials. Conducts Electricity. NOT to be used on live electrical or oil fires.
Dry Powder Colour: Blue	Extinguishes the flames over flammable liquids and small fires in solid materials. Re-ignition may occur in overheated liquids, such as hot bitumen. Non-conductor of electricity. May be used on live electrical equipment.
Foam Colour: Cream	Limited cooling. Forms a blanket over flammable liquids. Gives better control over re-ignition than dry powder and is well suited to extinguish fire in overheated liquids such as bitumen boilers and oil tanks. Conducts electricity. NOT to be used on live electrical equipment.
Carbon dioxide Colour: Black	Flammable liquids and electrical fires. Provides faster extinction of flammable liquid fires than a foam blanket would, but does not give as effective control over re-ignition. Do not use in confined spaces.

4. HAND TOOLS – SAFE USE AND HANDLING

4.1 Safe Storage

Injuries occur when hand tools fall from height, are tripped over, or placed in such a position that the cutting edge causes injury.

Hand tools must be stored in a safe manner.

- **Storage** – use boxes or other suitable containers. Where appropriate, hang tools from racks.
- **Protection** – make sure all cutting edges, teeth, etc. are adequately sheathed or otherwise protected.
- **Use** – do not lay tools down so that they can fall, roll or be knocked over or leave tools laying in walkways etc. where they present a tripping hazard.

4.2 Electrically Operated Tools

Every year there are fatalities and injuries on construction sites involving electricity.

Those using electrically operated hand tools must be trained and instructed in the correct and safe use of each tool.

The following check list is a helpful reminder of the key precautions:

- **Checking** – before taking possession of a tool check for any signs of damage to the tool itself or the electrical supply cable etc.
- **Reporting** – report any damage immediately and do not use the tool. Supervisors should arrange for defective equipment to be kept where it cannot be used until repaired.
- **Inherent safety** – make sure tools are either double-insulated or properly earthed with the correct fuses.
- **Lower voltage supply** – 110V supply should always be used on temporary wiring installations. In this case, approved waterproof socket outlets, plugs and distribution boxes must be used.

Hand Tools – Safe Use and Handling

- **Common dangers** – connections must be made using proper electrical connectors. Do not allow cables or wires to come into contact with moisture and do not carry or drag a tool by its cable. Cables and wires should be kept out of the way of others to avoid damage or a tripping hazard.

- **Setting up** – use electricity operated hand tools at the correct speed setting for the work and use the correct drill or blades. Check that chucks are secured.

- **Isolation** – disconnect tools from the power supply when not in use and before changing blades, discs and drill bits.

- **Vibration** – can cause diseases e.g. hand-arm vibration syndrome (HAVS). Take regular breaks when using vibratory tools. The safe period of operation for any vibrating tools should be assessed and the work organised to manage the risk e.g. by rotating tasks amongst the workforce. Examine your hands regularly and report any unusual tingling or loss of feeling.

- **Maintenance** – regular maintenance of electricity operated tools is essential and must be undertaken by a person who is properly trained. Temporary repairs by amateurs can be very dangerous.

- **Inspection and testing** – electrically operated tools should be inspected and tested at regular intervals by someone who is properly trained. A record of the inspection should be made.

- **First Aid** – make sure you have read and understood posters giving information on how to deal with electric shock, and the use of suitable fire extinguishers in case of an electrical fire. Do not touch anyone who appears to have suffered an electric shock unless you are sure that the power supply is dead.

4.3   Air Operated Tools and Equipment

Compressed air and associated hoses and tools can all be lethal if mishandled.

People required to use air operated equipment must have been instructed in safe use by a competent person.

The following basic rules below will help avoid accidents to yourself or others.

- **Hazard** – low compressed air pressures have been known to cause serious injuries or fatalities. Treat all compressed air systems and equipment with respect.

- **Checks** – before starting work check that hoses and pipes are not leaking.

- **Hoses** – keep hoses as short as possible, and away from traffic, where necessary by use of physical barriers. Do not bend or restrict hoses in any way to reduce power. Raised pressure on couplings may cause 'hose whip' and twist at high speed. Use whip-checks where are available to avoid being struck by hoses.

- **Misuse** – never direct the air jet at yourself or another person. Compressed air in the bloodstream, eyes, ears or nose can be fatal. Do not blow dust, swarf, etc. from clothing with an airline.

- **Emergencies** – make sure you have been instructed on the correct action to take if the airline breaks.

- **Isolation** – never try to change tools without turning off the air supply. Tools must be disconnected from the air supply for inspection and cleaning / maintenance or when not in use.

- **Inspection** – all equipment must be inspected weekly by someone who is properly trained, and a report must be kept on the inspection. The equipment must be kept clean and well maintained.

Hand Tools – Safe Use and Handling

- **PPE** – eye protection, gloves and/or protective footwear must be worn. In addition to other mandatory PPE (e.g. safety helmets) required on the site.

- **Noise** – air operated equipment should be properly silenced. Use any hearing protection provided for this purpose.

- **Vibration** – from air operated hand tools can cause HAVS. See Section 4.2 above.

4.4   Cartridge Assisted Tools

Cartridge assisted tools must be treated with the same respect as any fire-arm.

Persons using a cartridge assisted tool must be checked for colour blindness so they can identify cartridge strengths.

The users should undertake appropriate training and be formally authorised to use the tools.

Use the checklist below to make sure that you have not forgotten any important safety measure.

- **Risk to others** – remember that the risks in cartridge-assisted tools are primarily in relation to persons other than the user.

- **Authorised** – users must be authorised to use tool and sign for the number and type of cartridges issued.

- **Basic checks** – check immediately that the tool is not loaded. When inserting a cartridge, always point the barrel in a safe direction away from yourself or any other person. NEVER place your hand over the end of the barrel. NEVER walk about the site with a loaded tool. Always load the tool at the place of use. Hold the tool at right angles to the job when firing. Wear a safety helmet, eye protection and ear protectors when using the tool. When using pins for fixing through pre-drilled holes, make sure that a special adaptor is used - which will ensure that the pin is guided safely to its place of contact.

- **Power** – be aware of the possibility of the pin being fired through the material into which it is being fixed. Carry out tests to establish the correct strength of cartridge. Make sure no one is allowed behind the material into which the pin is being fixed during these tests.

- **Explosion risk** – the tool must not be fired in a place where flammable vapour or dust creates the risk of an explosion.

- **Misfire** – in the event of a misfire, wait one minute before unloading. Extract the cartridge in accordance with the manufacturer instructions. Do not use a screwdriver, nail or knife for this purpose. Misfired cartridges should be immersed in water to render them harmless.

- **Care and maintenance** – after use clean and oil the tool. Carry out routine maintenance and the replacement of worn parts that are interchangeable. The manufacturer must undertake all major repairs.

- **Cartridge storage** – stocks of cartridges must be stored in a damp-proof and flameproof box or cupboard which can be securely locked.

4.5   Power Saws

Those persons required to use power saws must be:

- Trained – for the work being undertaken at or on the machine in question.
- Instructed – be sufficiently instructed in the dangers and precautions, the guards and other safety devices connected with that machine.

Only those working under the direct supervision of a properly trained and experienced person as part of their training are exempted from these limitations.

Hand Tools – Safe Use and Handling

The checklists below serve as a reminder to those trained persons using portable chain saws and hand-held circular saws.

4.5.1 Chain Saws

When preparing to use a chain saw, operators should check:

- All nuts, screws etc. are tight.
- The saw chain is correctly tensioned.
- The throttle cannot be squeezed unless the throttle lockout is pressed.
- The correct PPE is being worn, including leg protection, eye protection, hearing protection and boots or gaiters.

When starting a chain saw, operators should:

- Place the saw on level ground.
- Secure the saw firmly, e.g. put a foot on the rear handle base plate and a hand on the front handle.
- Set the controls as recommended by the manufacturer.
- Pull the starter cord firmly.

Once the saw has started, the operator should rev the throttle to warm up the engine and check:

- The saw chain stops moving when the engine revs return to idle.
- The chain brake is effective when applied at max revs.
- The engine continues to run when the saw is turned through 90 degrees in any direction.
- The stop switch works correctly.
- Lubrication to the guide bar and chain is working properly.

4.5.2 Hand-held Circular Saws

Before using the saw ensure that:

- The blade is of the correct type for the material to be cut.
- It is in good condition, with no cracks or damage, and if it is toothed, that the teeth are sharp.
- It is properly and securely fixed to the machine.
- It will rotate in the correct direction; the sharp edge of the tooth must cut upwards from bottom to top of the material when the saw is in use.
- Alternatively, if direction of rotation is marked on the face of the blade and the body of the saw, the marks are both in the same direction.
- The depth of cut is adjusted so that the saw blade only just projects through the underside of the material being cut.
- The guard that covers the saw blade below the shoe is operating properly and retracts as the blade enters the material.

Other safety points are:

- **NEVER** tie back the guard or render it inoperative while sawing.
- **NEVER** adjust guards while the saw blade is in motion or the machine connected to the power supply.
- **NEVER** operate the machine with a defective **ON/OFF** switch and never secure the switch in the **ON** position.
- Always ensure that the supply cable is sufficiently long and so restrained that the saw cannot damage it before starting to cut.
- Whenever possible cut to a fence or guide to minimise the risk of the saw binding in the cut.

4.6   Drills

Drills may be powered by electricity or compressed air. Consider the risks which have been identified earlier for these power sources. Drills may simply rotate or rotate with percussion. In either case, bit should be sharp and clean and correctly fitted to the drill.

When drilling, operatives should wear the correct PPE to avoid materials entering their eyes or respiratory system. Hearing protection is also usually needed.

Operators should be aware that drills can cause hand-arm vibration syndrome (HAVS) and be aware of the characteristics of the drill so as to manage exposure time.

4.7   Breakers

Breakers are either powered by compressed air or electricity. The main risk is hand-arm vibration syndrome (HAVS) and operators must be aware of permissible operating time and management measures (e.g. job rotation/rest periods etc.).

Operators must wear suitable PPE, usually including eye protection, ear protection and respiratory protection. Many breakers are heavy and can be a cause of muscular skeletal disorders.

Always consider if it is possible to find remote machine options to use instead of hand held breakers.

4.8   Compactors

Hand held compactors are most often used for small amounts of backfilling such as trench backfilling. Larger areas should be compacted by rollers wherever possible.

Risks with compactors are similar to those using a hand-held breaker.

Key risks are hand-arm vibration, muscular skeletal disorder and noise. Operators should be properly trained and ensure that equipment is in good condition.

4.9 Abrasive Wheels

Abrasive wheels can cause fatal and serious accidents due to the misuse, mishandling or failure to select the correct wheel (or disc) for a particular operation.

Person mounting any abrasive wheel should be adequately trained and competent to do so. It is essential that operators and those responsible for wheel mounting should be able to recognise the specification marked on wheels.

The check lists below provide a reminder of what is needed to keep the operation safe.

4.9.1 Wheel Mounting

- Disconnect from mains before changing wheels and discs.
- Check all wheels for cracks and other damage before mounting.
- Check machine speeds against approved operating speed of the wheel.
- Use blotters supplied with the wheels.
- Make sure that the wheel hole, threaded or plain, fits the machine arbor properly and that flanges are clean, flat and of the proper type for the wheel you are mounting.
- Do not use excessive pressure when mounting the wheel between flanges. Tighten nut only enough to hold the wheel firmly.
- Do not use relieved or recessed flanges with threaded hole wheels, cones or plugs.
- Do not mount more than one wheel on a single arbor.

- Do not use a grinding wheel that has a rated speed less than the speed of the grinder.

4.9.2 Operating

- Always run the wheel in a protected area at least one minute before grinding.
- Always use the wheel guards furnished with the machine and ensure that they are properly fitted.
- Always wear protective safety glasses or proper face shield.
- Do not use wheels that have been dropped or otherwise damaged.
- Do not handle the machine carelessly. Racks or hooks should be used to support machines when not in use.
- When using portable grinding equipment keep clear of obstructions.

5. WORKING WITH PLANT

5.1 Goods Hoists

Incidents involving goods hoists usually arise from faulty erection, inadequate maintenance, misuse or failing to observe safe systems of work.

A hoist should not be operated by a person under the age of 18 unless they have the necessary maturity and competence, which includes having successfully completed appropriate training. During training they may use such equipment if they are adequately supervised.

Hoist users must always comply with the following check points:

- **Authorised** – only authorised persons may operate a hoist.

- **Defects** – do not operate a hoist if there is any defect present e.g. mechanical damage, safety device not working, or defects on the fencing or gates. Any such defect must be reported immediately to the supervisor. Do not interfere with any safety devices or bypass the devices.

- **Operating position** – you may only operate the hoist from one position. This must be located so that you can see the platform throughout its travel and have a clear view of each landing space.

- **Loading** – the safe working load must be clearly displayed and you must ensure that it is not exceeded. Make sure that loads are secure on the platform with special provision for preventing the movement of wheelbarrows. Consider how the load will be loaded and unloaded to avoid having to have people standing on the platform.

- **Passengers** – must NOT be carried on the platform.

- **Communication** – make sure you have a clear and distinct communication system with persons using the hoist.

- **Safe use** – All gates to the hoistway must be kept closed except when access to the stationary platform is required. You must not move the platform from the base of the hoistway, or any landing place, until the gate at that point is closed and you receive a signal to do so. Do not leave a hoist unattended with the motor running or switched on, or with the platform aloft. Make sure safe load notices are not obstructed or obliterated.

5.2   Dumpers

Small dumper accidents are often caused wholly or partly by driver error arising from inadequate training and inexperience.

If you are required to drive a dumper you MUST be properly trained and authorised to drive the vehicle. If required to drive on public roads, you must have a full driving licence and the vehicle must be licensed and equipped for the public highway.

Use the following checklist to help secure safe working:

- **Pre-start checks** – before operating check tyre pressures, oil, water, brakes, and that lights or mirrors fitted are in working order. Report all defects immediately.

- **Safe driving** – drive the machine with due consideration for others especially those working with or near you. Never carry passengers and steer the dumper with great caution.

- **Loading and tipping** – during loading engage the handbrake and disengage the gears. Do not remain in the seat. Stand well clear. The machine should be on level and stable ground. When tipping into excavations the wheels should be chocked to avoid any possible danger of the machine falling into the opening.

- **Capacity and visibility** – ensure that all loads are secure, evenly distributed and within the load-carrying capacity of the machine. Consider any inclines on the route of the dumper when calculating the load and stack loads so that forward vision is not impeded.

- **Skip safety catch** – make sure that the skip safety catch is engaged before moving off or when the dumper is left unattended.

- **Overturning** – avoid harsh acceleration and braking. Do not allow driving wheels to spin. Excessive speed and lock can lead to accidents. On down gradients always use lower gears and never travel across steep banks. Lack of stability on slopes is the most common cause of overturning. Always drive with care particularly on roadways with excessive camber. Take special care when carrying overhanging loads and use stop blocks for unloading next to spoil heaps and excavations.

- **Pedestrians** – before tipping make sure that no person or obstruction is in any danger.

- **Parking** – always park on level ground with the handbrake applied. Leave in neutral gear and chock the wheels if necessary. Never leave the dumper unattended with the engine running or the keys in the ignition.

- **Seat belts** – always fasten any seatbelt or other restraint device securely whilst driving. At the end of the normal working hours the machine should be effectively immobilised.

5.3   Cranes and Other Lifting Equipment

5.3.1   LOLER

Cranes and lifting equipment are subject to Lifting Operations and Lifting Equipment Regulations 1998(LOLER) which requires that lifting equipment provided for use at work complies with the following essential requirements, namely:

- **Strength** – is strong and stable enough for the particular use and marked to indicate safe working loads.

- **Positioned** – is positioned and installed to minimise any risks.

- **Operated** – is used safely, i.e. the work is planned, organised, carried out and supervised by competent people.

- **Examined** – subject to ongoing thorough examination by a competent person and

- **Inspected** – inspected at suitable intervals between thorough examinations.

The Regulations require that lifting operations must be planned, supervised and be carried out safely by competent people.

Those responsible for lifting operations have a legal duty to ensure compliance with the following requirements:

- **Planning and supervision** – lifting operations must be planned, supervised and carried out in a safe manner by people who are competent.

- **Periodic examination** – before lifting equipment (including accessories) is used for the first time it must be thoroughly examined. Lifting equipment needs to be thoroughly examined in use at periods specified in the Regulations i.e. at least six-monthly for accessories and equipment used for lifting people and, at a minimum, annually for all other equipment. All examination work should be performed by a competent person.

- **Examination reports** – Following a thorough examination or inspection of any lifting equipment, a report is submitted by the competent person to the employer to take the appropriate action.

Some people will be required to carry out work with lifting equipment as either a banksman or as a consequence of a particular duties.

Each situation needs separate consideration as outlined below.

5.3.2 Requirements for Banksmen

To be employed as a banksman you must be:

- over 18 years of age.
- medically fit with particular emphasis on eyesight, hearing and reflexes.
- good at judging distances, heights and clearances.
- agile and strong enough to handle lifting gear.
- trained in the general principles of slinging.
- trained in the selection of the correct lifting gear for loads to be lifted.
- aware of the safe working loads at the various radii of the crane with which you are working and aware when the crane approaches the safe radius for the load it is carrying.
- capable of directing the safe movement of the crane and its load, to maintain the safety of all personnel.
- thoroughly trained in a hand-signalling system familiar to the driver, or capable of giving clear and distinct instructions over radio and similar signalling systems.

Always obey the following operational precautions - both in your own interest and the safety of those around you.

- Only the official banksman should give instructions to the driver and except in an emergency, you should always pass on instructions via the banksman. The banksman should be easily identified by the colour of a high-visibility vest or helmet. For large cranes and for complex lifts, it is desirable for the banksman and driver to have radio communication.
- Beware of the crane's tail swing at ground level and the possibility of being trapped between the crane and any adjacent obstruction.

- Do not deliberately 'swing' loads to try and increase the radius of load deposit/pick-up.
- When assessing the weight of loads for lifting, remember the weight of the lifting gear must be added.
- Make sure that the lifting gear used is appropriate to the situation.
- When guiding mobile or crawler cranes from one location to another watch out for:
  - backfilled trenches that may settle under the crane load and cause it to topple over,
  - large obstructions on the ground,
  - overhead obstructions - particularly overhead power lines. (If travelling under such wires is necessary, wooden goalposts should be erected at safe distances from the wires, and all other ways under the wires blocked off). You should ensure that a competent person has assessed the gap required between the jib and any live power lines to avoid any power jumping the gap. Remember to allow for cambers and uneven ground.
- Make sure that no obstructions exist when slewing the crane - particularly electric cables of all types.
- If at any time in the work cycle you cannot see the driver, call for assistance, unless radio communication is used.
- Ensure that the load path does not pass over other workers or members of the public.

5.3.3 Working Near Cranes

If you have to work in association with a crane or you are working within the radius of a crane, it is in your own interests and those of your co-workers to be on your guard and observe the safety rules which should be agreed prior to commencing work.

- Keep clear of the tail swing of mobile and crawler cranes. It is easy to forget and be struck or crushed between the crane and an adjacent building or obstruction.
- Avoid standing under the load.
- While waiting for materials, concrete skips, formwork etc. to be swung into position, never turn your back on the load - always keep the load in your vision.
- In windy conditions, beware of formwork or other light but large area items being spun in the wind. There may be a need for guide ropes to control these loads.
- Never signal to the driver - that is the job of the banksman.

5.4 Working With Excavators

When carrying out work in association with excavators there is a serious risk that you might be struck by the boom or crushed between the counterweight and a fixed structure or other item of plant

Remember that, with modern hydraulic machines, all motions - dig, slew, raise boom, etc. - are much faster than non-hydraulic equipment.

Always observe the following basic rules:

- **Boom and counterweight** – the tail swing and the boom swing can be sudden and lethal if you are in the way. Stand well clear of both the operating boom and the tail swing.
- **Drivers dismount** – if you drive a lorry or dumper being loaded by an excavator, you must not remain on the vehicle while loading takes place. Stand well clear.

- **See and be seen** – always face excavating machinery and never turn your back on the plant. This is particularly important if you are in a supported trench and the excavator is removing the loose material for you. Never stand under the load when using the excavator as a crane. See below.

- **Excavation stability** – do not work in an unsupported trench unless a competent and experienced person declares it safe e.g. in solid rock or with trench sided battered back to a safe angle.

- **Lifting with excavators** – when excavators are used as for lifting it is important not to exceed the Safe Working Load (SWL) which should be marked on the machine. When working the excavator as a crane make sure that suitable slings and fixing points are used and that the slinging method has been carried out properly. Excavators can only be used for lifting weights in excess of 1000kg if they are fitted with capacity limiters or indicators, and hose burst check valves.

- **Communication** – if more than one person is working with an excavator, agree with the driver on who will be responsible for signals and instructions. Make sure you have good all round visibility.

5.5   Compressors

The main risks associated with compressors are being trapped and injured in the motor belt and pulley drive, explosions of the air receiver and accidents due to misuse of airlines.

Other possible risks are those of electric shock, burns from hot surfaces, slips resulting from oil spillage, and hearing damage through exposure to excessive noise.

5.5.1 Starting-up

If you are in charge of a compressor the following checklist should be used:

- Have all necessary maintenance checks been completed (the written scheme of examination will give the details)?
- Is the air receiver marked with its safe working pressure and distinguishing number? Is this pressure greater than the maximum pressure rating of the compressor? If not, has a reducing valve been fitted to prevent the safe working pressure of the receiver being exceeded?
- Is the air receiver fitted with a safety valve, pressure gauge, drain cock and manhole? Are they in working order?
- Is the compressor sited on level ground in a well-ventilated location, with no risk of exhaust fumes sinking into trenches, excavations or enclosed spaces nearby?

5.5.2 Operating

When operating the compressor check compliance with the checklist below:

- Avoid causing any damage to gauges and pressure relief devices. If damage occurs, shut the compressor down and report damage immediately.
- Pressure gauges must be kept clean and functioning correctly. If the safe working pressure is seen to be exceed at any time, shut down the equipment and report immediately.
- V-belt drive guards and those to other parts of the compressor must be firmly fixed in a position.
- If the compressor overheats, it must be stopped and the condition reported at once.
- Never use flammable liquids to clean any part of a compressor.

Working with Plant

If you are also required to use air operated equipment, see Section 4 for guidance.

5.6   Rough Terrain Forklifts and Telescopic Handlers

Rough terrain forklift and telescopic handlers require a thorough understanding of their individual characteristics if they are to be operated safely, especially factors affecting the vehicle stability.

If you are to drive such a machine you should:

- be aged 18 years or over,
- be in possession of a valid driving licence. (If your duties require you to operate on the public highway a driving licence is obligatory), continued
- be medically fit, with good eyesight, hearing and reflexes,
- have been adequately trained in the safe operation of the type of forklift truck you will be driving and be authorised to drive,
- have sufficient knowledge of the working of the machine to assure yourself that it is in full working order and to carry out daily maintenance.

Remember that additional training will be needed if you have to change machine type - especially if you change from forklift to telescopic handler or vice versa.

The following checklist will remind trained drivers of the key points in maintaining safe working practices.

- **Authorisation** – only operate the machine(s) for which you have received training and are authorised to use.
- **Daily checks** – carry out the laid-down daily maintenance and test overall serviceability before use. Report any defects and do not use the machine until it is put right.

- **Passengers** – never allow passengers to ride on any part of the forklift or handler.

- **Seat belt** – always fasten any seat restraint during use.

- **Machine limits** – understand the limits of your machine, both loaded and unloaded. Never exceed the maximum weight rating for the base machine or whatever authorised attachment is employed.

- **Stability** – always load with the mast vertical or tilted slightly back. To give maximum stability adjust forks to the widest spacing possible in relation to the load to be lifted.

- **Visibility** – try to ensure that the load does not obscure your view. If obstruction cannot be avoided either travel in reverse or use a banksman to guide you. Ensure you have sufficient mirrors for safe movement.

- **Pedestrians** – when manoeuvring and travelling beware of other people in the vicinity. Make use of your horn when necessary to warn others of your approach. You should use designated routes and management should separate pedestrians from any vehicle or plant movements.

- **During travel** – avoid sharp obstacles and badly uneven surfaces as far as possible - particularly backfilled installations. Always travel with the load in the lowest practicable position. Do not raise the load whilst travelling. Wait until the offloading position has been reached.

- **Off-loading** – deposit all loads carefully onto storage areas or loading platforms and avoid dragging the load when extracting the forks.

- **Speed** – drive your machine at a steady speed consistent with the site conditions and the loads being carried.

- **Slopes** – when driving on slopes see that the load is always facing uphill. If the forklift is not loaded, the forks should face downhill with the tilt adjusted to suit the gradient. Raise the forks just enough to clear the ground. Never cross slopes sideways.

- **Obstructions** – always check that there is enough clearance from overhead obstructions when the mast is extended. Take particular care near overhead power lines. Do not pass under the lines unless proper crossing points are provided with 'goalposts'.

- **Parking** – when parking the machine lower the forks to the ground. Remove the ignition key and apply hand brake effectively.

5.7 Woodworking Machinery

Woodworking machines are a frequent cause of serious injury including amputations. The legislation sets out safe methods of working with such machines in the Approved Code of Practice: Safe Use of Woodworking Machinery (ACoP).

Under the ACoP a woodworking machine can only be operated by a person who:

- has been sufficiently trained for the work being done at or on the machine in question,

- has been sufficiently instructed in the dangers and precautions, the guards and other safety devices connected with that machine,

- understands the requirements of the ACOP.

All operators must be competent to handle the equipment they are using. In addition, if they are under 18 years old, they must have successfully completed an approved training course if required to operate:

- a circular sawing machine,

- other machines fitted with circular saw blades,

- a surface planning machine when hand fed,

- a vertical spindle moulded.

Only those working under a properly trained and experienced person as part of their training are exempted from the above limitations.

As a reminder of instructions given during training, the following check list should be used regularly:

- **Awareness** – concentrate at all times. Distraction can be deadly. Do not leave a machine running and unattended.

- **Guards** – make use of all guards and make sure they are correctly adjusted.

- **Maintenance** – keep cutters and blades sharp, Check they are the right size for the machine and securely fixed.

- **Feeding** – use automatic feeding units, jigs or holders wherever possible. Do not feed timber into a circular saw without using a push stick. Support the free ends of long work pieces on trestles, table extensions etc.

- **Work area** – keep the area around machines clean and clear of wood chips and off cuts, etc. do not operate the machine in poor light.

- **Emergency stop** – check that you can easily reach the emergency stop control.

- **Cleaning** – do not attempt to clean or adjust a machine while it is running.

- **Hand held power saws** – do not use a portable hand held saw without first checking that the blade is in good condition, is properly fixed in the machine and rotates in the correct direction. Check the ON/OFF switch on a hand held saw before use and never secure the switch in the ON position.

- **Lighting** – do not operate a machine in poor lighting conditions

- **Noise** – use hearing protectors if they are provided for your use.

5.8   Small Site Concrete/Mortar Mixers

These items of plant are common features of the building site and frequently driven/operated by unskilled personnel selected from the site labour force.

Persons selected for these tasks should follow the basic rules below:

- **Instruction and training** – you must have been given adequate instruction and training by a competent person and authorised to use the mixer.

- **Guards** – check that all moving parts have proper guards securely fixed in place.

- **Location** – make sure that the mixer is properly set up level on firm ground or on a specially provided support system.

- **Maintenance** – the skip rope, drum and pulley gear, where used, should be properly maintained and regularly inspected. Safety chains must be fitted to supply skip to prevent it falling if the rope fails.

- **Loading** – if loading with a shovel, ensure that the shovel does not enter the bowl where it could be entangled with moving parts. Do not allow anyone to pass under the drum or supply skip. If mechanical loading is used barriers should be provided to keep others away from danger.

- **Cleaning** – keep the mixer and associated equipment in a clean and serviceable condition at all times. Do not hammer the drum or supply skip to clear material.

- **Stability** – make sure that the wheels are securely chocked to prevent movement.

- **Fumes** – if the plant is driven by an internal combustion engine make sure that exhaust fumes are well ventilated and cannot sink into trenches, excavations or other enclosed spaces where others are working.

5.9   Site Vehicles and Site Layout

Accidents involving plant and vehicle movements on construction sites are the second highest killer after falls from height.

All sites require a considered traffic management plan

Always remember the following:

- **Layout** – plan the layout of site cabins and stores to avoid vehicles coming onto site wherever possible and so that the need to reverse is minimised.
- **Parking** – plan site car parking to avoid crossing the site.
- **Segregation** – whenever possible, segregate plant and vehicles from pedestrians. This is particularly important to control members of the public who may have access (e.g. a supermarket car park where the supermarket continues to trade whilst being expanded).
- **Visibility** – ensure that vehicles have good all round vision. Consider the use of special mirrors or CCTV.
- **Lighting** – make sure that the vehicle can be seen by use of suitable lighting.
- **Reversing etc.** – use banksmen where needed, particularly when reversing or travelling near other hazards e.g. excavations or power lines.

6. SPECIAL HAZARDS, RISKS AND SUBSTANCES

6.1 Demolition

Demolition work is one of the most dangerous operations on a construction project. The work varies from the controlled collapse of large structures, using explosives, to demolition of walls by hand.

Suitable and sufficient steps must be taken to ensure that demolition or dismantling is planned and carried out under the supervision of a competent person.

Remote or distance demolition methods are best used where possible.

Always have a thorough understanding of the design and composition of the structure and where necessary obtain the advice of a suitably qualified structural engineer with experience of demolition works.

A full and project specific method statement for the operation will help ensure that the safe method of work established is communicated to those involved.

Follow these basic rules for safer demolition work:

- **Plan of work** – set out in writing the precise methods to be adopted. The timing and sequence should have been decided by a competent person before any work starts.

- **Briefing and instructions** – properly instruct all those involved in the above matters and never deviate from the sequence laid down unless authorised to do so.

- **Services** – before starting and while working take precautions (or confirm taken) to ensure that all services have been isolated and that there is no risk of flooding, electric shock or explosion from release or accumulation of gas.

- **Stability and support** – the plan of work must include such precautions as are necessary to prevent inadvertent collapse during the demolition. Be aware of the need for shoring or temporary support at any stage of the work. Do not make assumptions. Research available drawings and involve a structural engineer. Never remove any part of a structure unless you have been instructed to do so. Do not enter parts of a structure that refuse to collapse.

- **Confined spaces** – do not enter enclosed of confined spaces without proper authority and adequate precautions.

- **Report** – any unforeseen hazard to your supervisor immediately and warn your workmates.

- **PPE** – always wear a safety helmet and safety footwear and any other safety equipment that may be specified by management (gloves, goggles, masks etc.).

6.2   Asbestos

Asbestos causes the death of around 5000 workers each year. This number is more than the number of people who die in road traffic incidents each year. Around 20 workers in construction trades die each week as a result of past exposure to asbestos.

Asbestos is not just a problem of the past. It is present today in many buildings and other structures built or refurbished before the year 2000.

When materials that contain asbestos are disturbed or damaged, fibres are released into the air which can be inhaled and cause serious diseases. These diseases will not affect those exposed immediately since they often take a long time to develop. Once diagnosed it is often too late for any remedial action. This is why it is important that everyone takes steps to protect themselves now.

Special Hazards, Risks and Substances

The following key actions must be taken to minimise risk from asbestos:

- **Awareness** – information, instruction and training should be given to all workers and supervisors carrying out work which could disturb the fabric of a building, or other item which might contain asbestos. This is designed to help avoid working with asbestos. Do not work on such structures unless you have received such training etc.

This will not prepare workers to carry out work with asbestos-containing materials (ACMs). If a worker is planning to carry out work that will disturb ACMs, further information, instruction and training will be needed.

- **Assessment** – before starting any work that is likely to disturb asbestos, a suitable and sufficient risk assessment must be prepared by the employer. Whoever carries out the risk assessment must: be competent to do the risk assessment; carry it out before work begins and allow enough time to put appropriate precautions in place; and make sure the assessment is job specific and considers all aspects of the work.

The assessment must take account of any existing CDM health and safety file and the Pre-Construction Information provided by the client or principal designer.

Exposure – if you uncover or damage materials that may contain asbestos you must stop work immediately and arrange for the material to be tested. Meanwhile, keep everybody out of the area, minimise spread of any fibres and plan for personal and area decontamination.

When carrying out demolition, refurbishment or maintenance work you are quite likely to come across asbestos that has been used in:

- sprayed coatings for fire or thermal insulation,

- asbestos insulation lagging, in-fill or preformed sections for thermal, fire or acoustic purposes,
- asbestos insulating board,
- ceiling tiles and soffit boards,
- corrugated and flat sheeting,
- certain textured finishes,
- certain roofing felts and floor tiles.

The presence or absence of asbestos in many products and materials cannot be determined merely by observation. Analysis by specialists will be required.

IF YOU HAVE ANY DOUBT ABOUT THE MATERIALS YOU ARE WORKING ON - STOP WORK AND SEEK ADVICE IMMEDIATELY.

6.3   Lead Paint

Lead paint is much less used than it was in the past. However, work may take place on surfaces which were painted with lead based paint many years ago.

The rubbing down or scraping of the surface will produce dust containing lead which, if inhaled, could be dangerous. Where lead paint is suspected the risk should be assessed and appropriate precautions established.

A risk assessment must be undertaken where it is foreseeable that lead based paint is present and may be worked upon thereby giving rise to exposure to lead. Where lead is present suitable control measures must be established and communicated to all involved in the work.

Special Hazards, Risks and Substances

The following general rules should be followed to avoid damage to health.

- Rubbing down should be done using a wet process to minimise dust.
- Debris produced should be collected and removed to a safe place before it becomes dry.
- Burning old lead paint is dangerous. Lead poisoning can result from inhaling the fumes produced.
- Overalls should be worn during the working period and should be washed regularly.
- Adequate ventilation of the workplace is essential.
- Great care should be taken to wash adequately before eating, drinking or smoking.
- Use the protective equipment provided to you.

6.4 Dangerous and Hazardous Substances

A wide range substances which are dangerous e.g. LPG and / or hazardous to health e.g. solvent based paints, are widely used during construction work.

If you are involved in using or storing such materials, make sure you know and observe the rules for each type of gas, liquid etc.

6.4.1 Flammable Liquids

When exposed to the atmosphere, flammable liquids give off vapours (often heavier than air) which will accumulate at lower levels and be difficult to disperse.

These materials should be subject to a formal risk assessment before work starts to identify the scope for avoiding risk and the necessary precautions e.g. enclosure, powered ventilation and protected electrical equipment etc. to control the risk.

The precautions must be designed and effective to prevent build up and ignition of the vapours.

The product hazard data sheets should be observed and the following basic rules should be followed:

Storage

- Containers should preferably be stored in a securely fenced open air compound with a bund surrounding the drums. The bund should be capable of containing the contents of the largest drum stored plus 10%.

- Highly flammable liquids should never be stored with products such as oxygen (which could intensify any fire), LPG, or chlorine (which would add to the toxic hazards).

- No container should be stored nearer than 4 metres to any building or boundary fence.

- Drums should normally be stored upright. If stored horizontally, chocks must be used to prevent accidental movement. Any stacking must be stable.

- If it is necessary to store flammable liquids in a work room. The quantity must be kept to below 50 litres or a half days supply (whichever is the lesser), and all cans stored in cupboards or bins which are fire resistant.

- Any store must have a notice at the entrance boldly displaying the words "Flammable liquids". In addition, you must display prominent notices saying "No smoking" and "No naked lights".

- Check that containers are in good condition.

Special Hazards, Risks and Substances

Handling and use

- Keep containers in store until required for use, and return to store when no longer needed.

- Used drums should be treated with as much care as full ones because they will still contain flammable vapour.

- Transferring contents from large to small containers must always be done in the open air. Use funnels and spouts to prevent spillage. If spillage does occur, soak it up with dry sand and remove the contaminated sand to a safe place in the open air.

- If you cannot avoid using flammable liquids in an enclosed area, adequate forced ventilation should have been identified in the risk assessment.

- Use of flammable liquids may require special electrical arrangements for lighting, etc. to avoid any danger from electrical sources of ignition.

6.4.2   Liquefied Petroleum Gases (LPG)

Liquefied petroleum gases are butane and propane or any mixture of both. If there is a leak of liquid from a cylinder the liquid vapourises and, being heavier than air, will seep into drains, excavations and cellars.

The gas can travel considerable distances until reaching a source of ignition when it will set off a violent explosion which can flash back to the source of the leak.

LPGs can also produce a narcotic effect leading to asphyxiation if too much air is displaced. In any room where LPG is used for heating or cooking, there must be adequate ventilation.

There is a risk of asphyxiation if LPG-fuelled equipment is used in site huts without ventilation.

Storage

It is important to follow the rules given below.

- A suitable open air compound must be provided and used for storage. The cylinders must be kept at least 4 metres from the boundary fence, buildings and flammable materials. Keep the area free of all flammable material, weeds and rubbish.

- Never store cylinders below ground level.

- Do not store near excavations, drains and basements.

- Always keep cylinders upright, in use and storage.

- The valve must be kept closed when the cylinder is not in use.

- If you suspect a cylinder is leaking it must be moved to a safe position as soon as possible. Inform your supervisor at once.

- A dry powder fire extinguisher must be sited adjacent to any storage area.

- A prominent notice at the entrance to the compound "LPG - Highly flammable" plus notices prohibiting smoking and naked lights should be in place.

Site Usage

- Before use careful consideration must be given to the siting of LPG-fired appliances.

- The correct equipment must be used, and must include a regulator.

- Ensure that all joints are gas-tight. (Test with soapy water and a brush).

- Keep cylinders the recommended distance from the appliance.

- Ensure that the specified lighting procedures are used.

- Cylinders used for heating site huts must be outside the building.

- Adequate ventilation must be provided in huts.

- After use the cylinder must be turned off.

Special Hazards, Risks and Substances

Always seek advice if in doubt. Properly trained and competent fitters must carry out installation in huts etc.

6.4.3 Substances Hazardous to Health

A wide range of chemicals and materials which can harm the health of people are used in construction processes. Harm can be prevented if you know which chemicals are being used, the hazards they pose and how to manage those hazards and associated risks.

The Control of Substances Hazardous to Health Regulations 2002 (COSHH) require measures to control risks from hazardous materials.

To comply with COSHH you need to follow these steps:

Assess the risks	Assess the risks to health from hazardous substances used in or created by your workplace activities.
Decide what precautions are needed	You must not carry out work which could expose your employees to hazardous substances without first considering the risks and the necessary precautions, and what else you need to do to comply with COSHH.
Prevent or adequately control exposure	You must prevent your employees being exposed to hazardous substances. Where preventing exposure is not reasonably practicable, then you must adequately control it. The advice in this booklet and the other guidance referred to, will help you to make correct assessments and to put the appropriate controls into place.
Ensure that control measures are used and maintained	Ensure that control measures are used and maintained properly and that safety procedures are followed.
Monitor the exposure	Monitor the exposure of employees to hazardous substances, if necessary.

Carry out appropriate health surveillance	Carry out appropriate health surveillance where your assessment has shown this is necessary or where COSHH sets specific requirements.
Prepare plans and procedures to deal with accidents, incidents and emergencies	Prepare plans and procedures to deal with accidents, incidents and emergencies involving hazardous substances, where necessary.
Ensure employees are properly informed, trained & supervised	You should provide your employees with suitable and sufficient information, instruction and training.

For the vast majority of commercial chemicals, and materials such as paints and thinners, the presence (or not) of a warning label will indicate whether COSHH is relevant e.g. there will not be a warning label on ordinary washing-up fluid but there is one on bleach bottles.

Hazardous materials may be absorbed through the skin or swallowed (usually by eating or smoking with contaminated hands) or by breathing fumes or dust. Hygiene is very important and hands must be thoroughly cleaned after contact with hazardous materials.

Remember, the best way to prevent or adequately control exposure is to consider if it is reasonably practicable to do the following:

- Change the process or activity so that the hazardous substance is not needed.
- Replace hazardous materials with a safer alternative.
- Use material in a safer form, e.g. pellets instead of powder.

Special Hazards, Risks and Substances

If it is not practicable to carry out the above measures, exposure must be controlled by the following:

- **Process protection** – use appropriate work processes, systems and engineering controls, and provide suitable work equipment and materials e.g. use processes which minimise the amount of material used or produced or equipment which encloses the process so far as practicable.

- **Collective protection** – control exposure at source (e.g. local exhaust ventilation), and reduce the number of employees exposed to a minimum, the level and duration of their exposure, and the quantity of hazardous substances used or produced in the workplace.

- **Personal protection** – provide personal protective equipment e.g. face masks, respirators, protective clothing, as a last resort and never as a replacement for the other control measures above.

- **Health surveillance** – may be required if persons are exposed to certain hazardous substances linked to a particular disease e.g. respirable crystalline silica.

7. WORKING NEAR EXISTING SERVICES

7.1 Electricity

7.1.1 Overhead Power Lines

Contact with live overhead power lines can cause serious injuries and fatalities. This type of incident is particularly related to the use of excavators, lorry mounted and mobile cranes working or travelling near or under overhead cables.

The priority is to provide a safe place of work e.g. by arranging for power lines to be re-routed, switched off or protected by 'goalposts' and barriers.

If you have to work near overhead power lines observe the following basic rules:

- Treat all overhead lines as 'live' unless you have been specifically instructed otherwise.

- Know any minimum clearance requirements specified by the power line owner.

- Do not try to circumvent 'goalposts', barriers or other warnings.

- If you are a banksman always keep the overhead lines in view when giving directions, and only pass under where 'goalposts' are provided or it is clearly established that power has been turned off.

- If scaffolding is being erected adjacent to overhead lines, make sure that poles are handled a safe distance away. Notices should erected warning of electrical danger.

- Never stack materials or tip under overhead lines. This could reduce the safe clearance and, in wet weather and result in a 'flashover' to earth. The tipper body may come dangerously close to or touch the conductors with disastrous results.

- If work has to be carried out under the overhead conductors special precautions will be laid down by the power line owner.. Make sure you fully understand what is required.

Working Near Existing Services

- When working near power lines check that items of plant e.g. crane jibs cannot encroach on the safe clearance specified. Barriers should have been provided at an adequate distance to prevent this.

- Special rules apply to electricity powering railways where there could be a risk to trains in addition to workers. Consultation with the line owner must take place at an early stage.

7.1.2 Underground Cables

Damage to underground electrical cables can cause fatal or severe injury and you must take precautions to avoid danger.

This can be achieved by a safe system of work based on planning, use of plans, cable locating devices and safe digging practices. These four elements complement each other, and should all be used when working near buried cables.

- Planning the work
- Using cable plans
- Cable locating devices
- Safe digging practices

Injuries are usually caused by the explosive effects of arcing current and associated flames resulting in severe, potentially fatal, burns to the hands, face and body.

This can occur when a cable is: penetrated by a sharp object such as the point of a tool; or crushed severely enough to cause internal contact between the conductors or between metallic sheathing and one or more conductors.

The following explains what is required for safety near underground cables:

- **Planning the work** – The project client and principal designer must provide relevant information to designers and contractors about underground services so that they can plan the work to eliminate or reduce risks.

Most service cables belong to the regional electricity company. However, it is possible that some cables belong to other bodies e.g. highways authority, Ministry of Defence or Network Rail.

You may need to make dead for the work to proceed safely. Electricity companies are required to give five days' notice to customers whose supply is to be disconnected.

Careful planning is essential before the work starts. Risk assessments should consider how the work is to be carried out ensuring local circumstances are taken into account.

- **Using cable plan** – Plans or other suitable information about all buried services in the area should be obtained and reviewed before any excavation work starts.

Where it is not possible for those undertaking the excavation work to obtain information e.g. emergency work being undertaken, the work should be carried out as though there are buried services in the area.

Symbols on electricity cable plans may vary between utilities and advice should be sought from the issuing office. Remember that high-voltage cables may be shown on separate plans from low-voltage cables.

Plans give only an indication of the location, configuration and number of underground services at a particular site. Subsequent tracing by locating devices is essential.

- **Cable locating devices** – Before work begins, underground cables must be located, identified and clearly marked.

The position of the cable in or near the proposed work area should be pinpointed as accurately as possible by means of a locating device, using plans, and other information as a guide to the possible location of services and to help interpret the signal.

Remember: Locators should be used frequently and repeatedly during the course of the work.

People who use a locator should have received thorough training in its use and limitations. Locating devices should always be used in accordance with the manufacturer's instructions, regularly checked and maintained in good working order.

- **Safe digging practices** – Excavation work should be carried out carefully and follow recognised safe digging practices.

Once a locating device has been **used** to determine position and route, excavation may proceed, with trial holes dug using suitable hand tools as necessary to confirm the position.

Excavate alongside the service rather than directly above it. Final exposure of the service by horizontal digging is recommended as the force applied to hand tools can be controlled more effectively.

7.2   Gas, Water Mains and Sewers

Locating gas, water mains and sewers requires the same degree of care required in respect of electric cables. The utility owner should be contacted to determine where such services are on your project. The locations given should only be taken as approximate and more positive means used to fix their line more accurately.

A visual survey of the area should have been made to locate manholes, stop cock covers, hydrants and buried valves etc. An electro-magnetic pipe detector should be available to confirm locations although this will not locate plastic pipes.

Final confirmation must be secured by carefully dug trial holes. Those required to carry out such work should follow the guidance given below.

7.2.1 Gas Mains

When excavating near a gas main the following basic precautions should be observed:

- Remember that gas mains have a flammable and explosive content.

- Work with care and do not create a situation where joints may be strained.

- If the pipe has to be supported, ask to be briefed on the owner requirements before starting work.

- At the slightest hint of gas escape, leave the excavation and prevent anyone going near it. No naked lights must be allowed. Call the pipe owner immediately.

- Never use a gas main as a hand or foot hold.

- Do not drop tools or other weights onto mains, as many old mains are of cast iron and may crack if they are in poor condition.

- Modern smaller diameter house mains are often plastic, do not confuse them with electric cables.

- Owners of the system will have precise specifications in relation to back filling round mains. Make sure you have been properly instructed in this respect.

7.2.2 Water Mains

A water main does not usually involve the risk inherent in electricity and gas services. However, fracturing even a small water pipe can cause great inconvenience to householders and flood work areas.

Working Near Existing Services

If a large high pressure main is breached the results can be spectacular and very costly. A great deal of flooding can take place before the water supply is isolated an area the size of a small town left temporarily without water.

Breaking a high pressure main with power tools can cause injury as the tool is thrown by a powerful jet of water.

If the line of a main has been properly established by trial pits, stop cock locations etc., and you have to carry out excavations in the vicinity, you should:

- Be aware of any supporting of the main that is required.
- Work adjacent to and around the pipe using hand tools with care.
- Do not confuse smaller plastic pipes with plastic sheathed electric cables.
- Follow the pipe owner backfilling specification.
- Call the owner of the pipe immediately if the main is damaged.

7.2.3   Sewers

Sewers should be located by tracing manhole covers and confirming the location of the sewer between the manholes. The main risk to health is if you are working in a trench and a foul sewer is damaged.

Leave the trench immediately to avoid the possibility of asphyxiation. Do not return until adequate ventilation has been provided and the area declared safe for work.

Report any damage to the sewer owner. If you break a storm water sewer and rain is falling vacate the excavation as it may flood from the sewer at any time.

7.3   Telecommunication Equipment

Telecommunications equipment on building structures introduces a hazard from Radio Frequency (RF) transmissions.

Trades that are particularly at risk are those who access the roof areas of non-domestic property to repair and maintain plant and equipment or undertake roof repairs and those e.g. scaffolders or rope access operative gaining access to other parts of the building structure.

When undertaking work in the vicinity of telecoms equipment the owner of the site or the operator of the equipment should be contacted prior to any work being carried out.

Exclusion zones are often marked out around antennas and other equipment, or are indicated on warning labels. If work within an exclusion zone is unavoidable arrangements MUST be made for the antenna to be powered down or for the antenna field strength to be reduced to a safe level.

Safe working conditions must be secured by locking or guarding the associated power controls, and by continuous monitoring of the field strength whilst the work is in progress.

8.   OCCUPATIONAL HEALTH MANAGEMENT AND FIRST AID

8.1   Introduction

There have been significant improvements over recent years in reducing the number and rate of fatal and other injuries involving construction workers. However, construction remains a high-risk industry regarding injury accidents. What is less understood is that construction is also a high-risk industry regarding the ill health caused by working on construction projects. .

Below are some key points about these risks to health and why they are so significant and how to manage them.

Ill-health picture

Every year more working days are lost due to work-related illness compared to injuries. The statistics reveal that construction workers have a high risk of developing diseases from a number of health issues.

- **Cancer** – construction has the largest burden of occupational cancer amongst the industrial sectors. It accounts for over 40% of occupational cancer deaths and cancer registrations. It is estimated that past exposures in the construction sector annually cause over 5,000 occupational cancer cases and approximately 3,700 deaths. The most significant cause of these cancers is asbestos (70%) followed by silica (17%) working as a painter and diesel engine exhaust (6-7% each).

- **Hazardous substances** – dusts, chemicals and potentially harmful mixtures (e.g. in paints) are common in construction work. Some processes emit dusts, fumes, vapours or gases into the air and these can be significant causes of breathing problems and lung diseases. A number of construction-related occupations also have high rates of dermatitis from skin exposures to hazardous substances.

- **Physical health risks** – skilled construction and building trades are one of the occupations with the highest estimated prevalence of back injuries and upper limb disorders. Manual handling is the most commonly reported cause of over seven day injuries in the industry. Construction also has one of highest rates of ill health caused by noise and vibration.

Underlying causes

There are many reasons why construction workers have a high risk of developing occupational disease. This includes:

- **The construction site environment** – unlike a factory, construction work takes place in many and varied environments. Different sites can present a range of health risks, including existing ones like asbestos. The extent of these risks can also vary between areas of the same site.

- **The dynamic nature of the work** – construction sites are constantly changing and a large number of trades may all be carrying out tasks potentially dangerous to their health and that of others.

- **Risk appreciation** – there is generally a low awareness of health risks and the controls needed. It can take many years for serious ill health conditions to develop and the immediate consequence of a harmful workplace exposure may often be dismissed as not significant compared to the immediate impact of injuries caused by accidents.

- **Employment** – many workers are either self-employed, work for small companies, or frequently change employers. Others work away from home. These situations can make it problematical for workers to easily look after their own health and they often have little or no contact with occupational health professionals.

8.1.1 Principles of Occupational Health Management

Managing occupational health should be an integral part of the company overall management system. Health on construction sites can be managed by use of management systems similar to those developed in order to manage safety issues.

This section introduces the principles of an occupational health management model which acts as a framework to enable everyone involved in the construction process to help to manage the risks which exist to the health of workers.

The process starts with the client and the design team who by specifying the design and materials used can actually help to eliminate or to reduce risks to health at the very start of the construction process.

The risk of ill health can be managed by following a few essential common principles:

- **'Ill-health can be prevented'** – it is possible and practical to carry out construction work without causing ill-health.

- **'Treat health like safety'** – managing health risks is no different to managing safety risks.

- **'Everyone has a role to play'** – everyone involved in construction has a responsibility in managing risks to health. Each must take ownership of their part of the process.

- **'Control the risk, not the symptoms'** – monitoring and health surveillance programmes are not enough on their own. While they are an effective part of managing health risks, the first priority is to stop people being exposed to the risk in the first place.

- **'Manage risk, not lifestyles'** – the law requires steps to be taken to prevent or adequately control work-related health risks. Helping workers tackle lifestyle issues like smoking or diet may be beneficial but is not a substitute for risk control in the workplace.

8.2   Occupational Health Risk Management System

The system can be illustrated by the following simple flow-diagram. It is important to remember MANAGE THE RISKS -NOT THE SYMPTOMS. This means seeking to identify and manage potential occupational health matters BEFORE they become a problem.

Occupational Health Policy

Identify Health Risks

Eliminate Risk Where Possible

Identify Who is at Risk or Residual Risks

Manage Residual Risks - via

| Entry Health Checks | Control Measures | Health Check | Back to Work |

8.2.1   Policy

Policy should consist of the following:

- A general statement on Policy.
- Organisation.
- Arrangements.

8.2.2   Identify Health Risks

Consider what risks exist. The most common risks in construction arise from the following:

- Muscular Skeletal Disorder (MSD).
- Noise Induced Hearing Loss (NIHL).
- Hand Arm Vibration Syndrome (HAVS).
- Dermatitis.
- Stress.
- Respiratory Problems.

8.2.3 Eliminate Risks Where Possible

Once you have identified the health risks relevant to your construction activities, then you should eliminate as many as possible. This will save you time and effort, as you will not need to take any further action in relation to these risks.

For example, you could eliminate the risk by:

- Replacing a dangerous substance with one which is safe to use.
- Using lifting aids to avoid manual handling.
- Using specialist pile cap removal techniques in place of hand held breakers to avoid hand arm vibration and excessive noise.
- Using pre-fabricated cladding panels and lifting aids to avoid dermatitis from the use of wet cement and MSD injuries to bricklayers.

8.2.4 Identify Who is at Risk to the Residual Risks

Think of the activity, the risks, the location and who could possibly be affected.

You should also take into account the health of the worker carrying out the tasks. For example, a worker showing signs of early stages of HAVS should not be put to work on vibrating tools without proper consideration and controls. As another example, a tower crane driver with un-corrected poor eyesight would put himself and others at risk.

8.2.5 Manage Residual Risks

There are four key processes involved in managing occupational health risks. They are the following:

- Entry Health Checks (including Fitness for Work and Pre-Employment Screening, statutory medical examinations and health promotion).
- Risk Control.
- Ongoing Health Checks (including Health Monitoring, Health Surveillance and self checks).
- Back to work (including rehabilitation).

It is essential to recognise that occupational ill-health can lead to accidents if 'safety critical' people are not fully fit (e.g. a tower crane operator with defective sight).

8.2.6 Back to Work

Employers should have a policy of working with employees in order to get them back to work as soon as practicable and safe. This could involve help in medical treatment or re-assessing the tasks which can be done until full health is regained. In practice it will usually be necessary to involve insurers for any significant incident.

8.3 Common ill health risks in Construction

Construction workers are exposed to physical ill health risks from noise, vibration, manual handling and doing repetitive tasks. The workforce is also exposed to many different types of hazardous substances such as dust, lead or cement.

8.3.1 Physical ill health risks

The key physical risk health effects in construction are:

- **Musculoskeletal Disorders (MSDs)** – MSDs are injury, damage or disorder of the joints or other tissues in the upper / lower limbs or the back. Skilled construction and building trades are one of the occupations with the highest estimated prevalence of back injuries and upper limb disorders. Handling is also the most commonly reported cause of over seven day injuries in the industry.

- **Noise Induced Hearing Loss (NIHL)** – noise is part of everyday life but construction has one of the highest rates of occupational deafness. Too much noise can cause permanent and disabling hearing damage. This often takes the form of hearing loss that gets worse over time but damage can also be caused by sudden, extremely loud noises. Regular frequent noise is also linked to tinnitus (permanent ringing in the ears).

Occupational Health Management and First Aid

- **Hand-Arm Vibration Syndrome (HAVS)** – HAVS is a range of conditions to the hands and arms caused by frequent exposure to vibration from hand-held power tools (such as grinders or road breakers) and hand-guided equipment (such as pedestrian controlled floor saws). This causes poor blood circulation, neurological and muscular damage to the affected areas and can permanently reduce the ability to grip properly. Construction has one of the highest rates of HAVS of all industries.

The risk of getting these ill health conditions is related to a number of common factors:

- **Who** – who is at risk? Think about your employees. Who is using noisy or vibrating equipment? Is anyone lifting heavy loads or doing repetitive tasks? Has health surveillance identified anyone with existing problems that could be made worse? Is there anyone else who might be affected by the noise you are making?

- **What** – what tasks are you doing? Some tasks, such as lifting blocks or kerbs can present specific dangers. The level of risk will also be influenced by how frequently someone is exposed and whether there is any variation during the day / over different days.

- **Where** – where the work is taking place can also have an effect. Small and enclosed spaces increase noise levels. Having to adopt awkward postures can increase the force needed to apply and control tools. This can increase the vibration levels passing into the user's hand and arm. Similarly, awkward postures place added strain on the body when lifting or carrying.

8.3.2 Hazardous substances

Hazardous substances come in a number of different forms:

- **Solids** – including particles of solid material that get into the air such as dust, fibres, smoke and fume.

- **Liquids** – including fine sprays, mists and aerosols made up of small droplets of liquid – e.g. sprayed paint.

- **Vapours** – gaseous forms of a liquid or solid, e.g. solvent vapour.
- **Gases** – some processes can generate gases like carbon monoxide or engine exhaust gases.
- **Micro-organisms** – microscopic organisms, like bacteria, viruses and fungi can be found almost everywhere.

Under certain conditions, a substance can exist in more than one form at the same time (e.g. paint spraying can produce fine mists of liquid droplets and also solvent vapour). Knowing the correct form(s) a hazardous substance takes is important for getting the right controls.

Hazardous substances can get into the body in a number of ways. There are three main routes:

- **Lungs and airways** – hazardous substances can be inhaled in the air you are breathing. The lungs and airways are vulnerable to many of these substances like dust or isocyanates. Your lungs are also closely linked to the circulatory system so the oxygen we breathe in the air can be transferred to the blood and on to all the tissues and organs in the body. This means that harmful substances, like solvent vapours, could also get into your blood and be distributed around your body.
- **Skin** – some substances, such as cement, can directly affect your skin through contact leading to problems like dermatitis or burns. Other substances, e.g. solvents, can be absorbed through your skin into the blood. Harmful micro-organisms can also get into your body through cuts and wounds.
- **Mouth** – everyone eats and drinks. Some people also smoke. You can therefore transfer hazardous substances into your body e.g. when eating or smoking with hands contaminated with lead dust.

Effects

Different substances can harm your health in different ways. Some of these occur more immediately, like dizziness, headaches and nausea from solvents or burns from cement. Others, such as lung diseases, can take much longer and sometimes many years to develop.

Occupational Health Management and First Aid

Construction is a high-risk industry for health issues. Hazardous substances cause many of these issues, particularly in relation to occupational cancers where the industry has the largest burden amongst the industrial sectors.

8.4   First Aid and Legal Requirements

The employer is required to provide proper equipment to enable first aid to be given to any employees who are injured or become ill at work. The workforce must be fully informed of the arrangements.

8.4.1   First Aid Boxes, Qualified First Aiders and Appointed Persons

Every construction site must have at least one first aid box which must contain first aid materials and nothing else. On extensive sites a number of boxes will be required. Each box must be placed in a clearly identified location. First aid box contents are listed below.

A risk assessment should be carried out to identify the number of qualified first aiders needed. Factors to consider include the numbers at risk, the nature and location of the work (e.g. working in a remote rural site against working in a hospital).

Employers have to provide appointed persons to take charge of first aid arrangements where the provision of a qualified first aider is not essential and where first aiders are absent because of exceptional and temporary circumstances e.g. illness.

8.4.2   First Aid Rooms

The provision of a first aid room must be considered for all large construction sites, for sites with special risks and where access to accident and emergency facilities outside the site is difficult.

If a first aid room is provided it should fulfil the following requirements:

- Be under the charge of a qualified first aider; names and locations of all the first aiders should be displayed. It is good practice for first aiders to be easily identified (e.g. by marking helmets).
- Be readily available and used only for the rendering of first aid.
- Be clearly identified and of sufficient size to allow access for a stretcher, wheelchair, etc., and to hold a couch with space for people to work around it.
- Contain in addition to the previously-mentioned first aid materials:
  - a sink with hot and cold running water.
  - drinking water.
  - an eye bath with sterile water.
  - paper towels, soap and nail brush.
  - smooth-topped, impermeable work surface.
  - clean garments for use by first aiders.
  - a couch with pillow and blankets frequently cleaned.
  - refuse container with disposable liner.
  - bags.
  - bowl.
  - chair.
  - accident book and treatment record.
- Be heated, lighted, ventilated and cleaned regularly.
- Be designed so that immediate contact can be made with the person on call, e.g. radio, siren, and a telephone link.

8.4.3 Stretchers and 'Supplementary Equipment'

Additional items of first aid equipment which may be provided are as follows:

- disposable gloves and aprons.
- cleaning wipes - alcohol free.
- stretchers.
- blankets.
- blunt ended stainless steel scissors.
- plastic bags for disposing of soiled dressings.

9.   WELFARE FACILITIES

The project client and contractors must both ensure that the welfare facilities required by CDM 2015 Schedule 2 are provided in respect of any person carrying out construction work on the project.

The minimum required standards in relation to welfare facilities include the following:

- toilet facilities kept clean, ventilated and properly lit (male and female);
- wash basins with hot and cold or warm running water (large enough to wash forearms properly), soap and towels or other drying facilities;
- changing facilities (male and female as appropriate) including areas for drying wet clothing and storing clothing;
- drinking water and a supply of cups or a water fountain; and
- warm place where workers can sit, make hot drinks and prepare and heat food. The place should be equipped with seating with backs.

When planning the layout of welfare facilities consider issues such as:

- setting up near the site entrance to avoid visitors, delivery vehicles etc. crossing the site to access offices and welfare facilities;
- vehicle routes established to segregate vehicles and pedestrians where practicable; and
- access onto and from the site for vehicles and pedestrians.

10. PERSONAL PROTECTIVE EQUIPMENT (PPE)

You can do a great deal to protect yourself simply by knowing what PPE is available, wearing the correct clothing and using the protective equipment appropriate to your job circumstances.

Remember that PPE should only be considered AFTER considering if hazards and risks can be eliminated or mitigated. PPE is a control measure for residual risks.

Employers are obliged by law to provide, without charge, personal protective equipment to any of their employees who may be exposed to a risk to their health or safety. Amongst the types of PPE which may be provided are the following:

- Safety helmets.
- Safety boots.
- Suitable gloves.
- Suitable protective clothing for persons working out-of-doors.
- Suitable protective clothing for person working with asbestos or asbestos-based materials.
- Insulating screens, boots and gloves to prevent danger of electric shock.
- Eye protectors or shields.
- Respirators or breathing apparatus – to avoid breathing injurious dust or fumes.
- Safety nets, harnesses, lines, etc., where it is not reasonably practicable to provide working platforms.
- Ear protectors where it is not reasonably practicable to reduce noise below an acceptable exposure level.
- Adequate protective clothing for employees liable to be exposed to significant levels of lead. At the same time, you as an employee are required by law to wear such clothing and equipment where the circumstances demand it.

For your further guidance, more detailed notes on the protection of various parts of the body are given in the following sections. Unless there are specific reasons, most responsible employers require workers to wear a helmet, a high-visibility vest or jacket and suitable footwear.

10.1   Types of PPE

10.1.1 Hands

Many of the hand injuries which occur every year would have been avoided, or would have been much less serious, if the correct industrial gloves had been worn.

Industrial gloves will also protect the hands from substances which can damage the skin such as certain chemicals regularly used on construction sites. The correct type of glove for the situation is essential as no glove gives protection from all possible hazards.

Suitable gloves should be used when, for example:

- Handling objects with sharp or rough edges, bricks, paving slabs, glass, etc.
- Handling wire ropes, etc., which could have broken strands,
- Unpacking banded loads where the bands can be very sharp,
- Work in dirty or contaminated areas,
- Using chemicals and other hazardous substances.
- Working with concrete or mortars.

Suitable gloves can help keep hands warm and maintain good blood flow which reduces risk of possible vibration injury.

10.1.2 Eyes

Probably one of the most traumatic accidents that can occur is a person being blinded at work. Such accidents should never happen, as there are specific legal requirements on employers to issue eye protection.

Equally, employees are required to use that protection. Either party, by not fulfilling their obligations, can be liable to possible legal proceedings.

The eye protection that is provided must be suitable for individual operatives and for tasks and must be replaced immediately if lost or damaged. Operatives must take care of the protection given to them. It is important to keep them clean and in good operating condition.

10.1.3 Feet

Injuries to the feet through treading on sharp objects such as nails or heavy items dropped on the feet, are always high on the annual figures for construction accidents.

Safety footwear is essential on construction sites, and will protect the feet from serious injury in most of the common types of site accidents. It comes in many different styles from fashionable shoes to heavy duty boots.

All styles have protective safety toecaps, and spring steel midsoles to protect the sole of the foot are incorporated if required. Rubber boots are also available with toecaps and midsoles. Plimsolls and soft shoes should never be worn on site.

10.1.4 Lungs

Many of the jobs that are involved in construction produce dust and others involve the use of substances which give off fumes. Many of these dusts and fumes are injurious to health, and are dealt with in the appropriate sections of this guide. Where protection is necessary and provided by using the correct type of respirator with the correct filter, it is in your interest to wear the equipment and make sure it is maintained, cleaned and the filters replaced on a regular basis. Where they are needed, respirators and masks will be provided by the employer.

In many instances respirator users will be need to undergo face fit testing to confirm that the respirator will be effective for the indivual user.

10.1.5 Ears

Excessive noise at work can cause serious damage to your hearing. In some cases an employer is required by law to protect operatives from the effects of noise, in others employers give protection on a voluntary basis. Whichever is the case, you should wear the hearing protection provided wherever and whenever it is considered necessary to safeguard your hearing. Hearing protection needs to be specific to protect against different forms of notice.

10.1.6 Backs

Back problems cause a great deal of lost time in the industry. Many back problems are not caused by lifting heavy loads but by constant exposure to wet and cold.

Employers will provide wet weather clothing, but it is up to you to dress correctly with warm clothing in cold weather, with special consideration being given to protecting the back. It is a good idea to have spare warm clothing to change into should you get wet.

Other sections of this booklet also give guidance on protective clothing appropriate to the specific item.

10.1.7 Safety Helmets

The head is particularly vulnerable to injury, and accidents to the head are often fatal or involve very serious injuries, such as brain damage or fractured skull.

Over the years it has been proved beyond doubt that many deaths and head injuries could have been prevented, or their severity reduced, by wearing safety helmets.

All workers must be provided with, and wear, suitable head protection. This is necessary to comply with the Personal Protective Equipment Regulations 1992 which applies to the provision and wearing of head protection on construction sites.

Personal Protective Equipment (PPE)

Site management is responsible for seeing that safety helmets which conform to the appropriate British Standard are made available. For maximum safety and comfort, follow the points given below:

- You should adjust the headband to suit your head size.
- Check that the outer shell and harness are in good condition, without indentations or cracks.
- Never paint the shell, as some paints weaken the plastics used.
- Only the recommended harness should be used to ensure proper clearance for deflection of the shell under the impact and for ventilation.
- Chin straps should be used to avoid the possibility of the safety helmet falling off when bending down, or in high winds.
- Holes must not be punched into the shell for attaching unauthorised equipment. Various attachments for ear defenders, eye protection or visors are available and should only be used in accordance with the manufacturers' instructions or advice.
- Any helmet should be replaced if it sustains a heavy impact, as the shell may be weakened locally and affect the strength of the helmet.

Note that whilst most tasks can be carried out safely with a standard helmet, special helmets are available for specific tasks such as abseil access.

10.2 Protection Against the Operations of Others

There will be times when work has to be carried out on the fringe of, or assisting persons carrying out, specialised processes. You should be aware of what protection you need in such cases. You may need to review this daily as changes or programme slippage may mean trades working closer together than originally planned.

10.2.1 Welding

- For assisting a welder, or working adjacent to his activities, you must wear goggles or a shield of the correct type to protect your eyes from infra-red or ultra-violet rays.

- If you are employed to carry out weld chipping, goggles must be worn to protect your eyes from flying pieces of slag.

- Where electric welding is carried out the work must be effectively screened to avoid harmful radiation to nearby workers.

- Reinforced leather gloves should be worn when handling hot welded elements and as a protection against sparks, molten metal and radiation.

10.2.2 Lasers

Lasers are now commonly used for setting out, levelling screeds, laying pipes to correct falls, etc. If you work with or near lasers remember:

- All lasers are dangerous if the eyes look directly into the beam,

- With pulsed lasers, eye injury can occur at great distances,

- They can also cause burning of the skin and blind spots on the retina of the eye due to destruction of the retina tissue,

- Where total enclosure of the beam is not possible, eye protection must be provided to you, suitable for the laser in question.

10.2.3 Site Radiography

If X-ray machines, Nuclear Density Gauges, or sealed sources (know sometimes as 'bombing') are being used on site, remember:

- Make yourself aware of the controlled area, and do not enter it without the authorisation of the Radiation Protection Supervisor (RPS).

- Check the local rules if you need to work in or near the affected area.

11. ACCIDENT REPORTING AND RECORDING

All injuries and dangerous occurrences must be reported promptly.

RIDDOR 2013 legislation ((Reporting of Injuries, Diseases and Dangerous Occurrences Regulations 2013) requires deaths and specified injuries etc. resulting from accidents, to be reported to the relevant enforcing authority. In construction this will be HSE (Health & Safety Executive) in nearly every case

The site manager must be informed as soon as practicable after any injury or dangerous occurrence has occurred. The statutory reporting and recording requirements as follows:

Reporting – The Reporting of Injuries, Diseases and Dangerous Occurrences Regulations 2013 (RIDDOR 2013) requires the recording and reporting to HSE of certain defined work related injuries, incidents and occupational diseases.

Recording – records must be kept of: injuries, occupational diseases or dangerous occurrences which require reporting under RIDDOR; AND any other occupational accident causing injuries that result in a worker being away from work or incapacitated for more than three consecutive days.

Your co-operation is therefore very important. If there is an accident at your workplace, help by:

- Making sure that first aid assistance is called immediately, in the case of serious injury.

- Seeing that it is reported without delay to your supervisor, even though no person has been injured or plant damaged.

- Ensuring, in the case of serious personal injury, that the accident site is left undisturbed until clearance is given by your supervisor or safety officer.

- Ensuring that any items which may assist in the accident investigation (e.g. damaged slings, broken abrasive wheels) are retained and passed to your supervisor.

12.   SAFETY SIGNS AND SIGNALS

Safety signs are governed by the health and safety regulations 1996. The Regulations cover various means of communicating health and safety information. These include illuminated signs, hand and acoustic signals in addition to the traditional signboards such as prohibition and warning. The following section gives some examples of the signs and signals you may come across on site.

12.1   Mandatory Signs

Warning Signs

Caution

Biohazard

Caution compressed gas

Caution corrosive substance

Caution fixed overhead hazard

Caution fork-lift trucks operating

Caution fragile roof

Caution slippery surface

Danger highly flammable

12.2   Warning Signs

Danger of electrocution

High noise levels

Radiation hazard

Risk of explosion

Warning overhead loads

12.3 Safety Signs

12.4   Fire Signs

12.5 Fire Extinguishers

12.6 Banksman Signals

OPERATIONS START
(FOLLOW MY INSTRUCTIONS)

STOP   EMERGENCY
            STOP

HOIST
CLENCH AND UNCLENCH
FINGERS TO SIGNAL
'INCH THE LOAD'

LOWER   LOWER
          SLOWLY

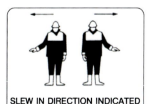

SLEW IN DIRECTION INDICATED

JIB UP   JIB DOWN

DERRICKING JIB
SIGNAL WITH ONE HAND
OTHER ON HEAD

12.6 Banksman Signals

EXTEND JIB   RETRACT JIB

TELESCOPING JIB
SIGNAL WITH ONE HAND
OTHER ON HEAD

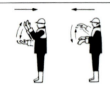

TRAVEL TO ME   TRAVEL FROM
ME

SIGNAL WITH BOTH HANDS

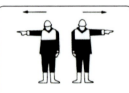

**TRAVEL IN DIRECTION
INDICATED**

HORIZONTAL   VERTICAL
DISTANCE   DISTANCE

OPERATIONS START
(ALTERNATIVE)

OPERATIONS CEASE
(ALTERNATIVE)

13   HOW TO GET MORE INFORMATION AND HELP

13.1   Health and Safety Executive (HSE) Publications

HSE guidance is available on all the subjects covered in this booklet. All are free to download from the HSE website: www.hse.gov.uk

All health and safety legislation can be found online at: http://www.legislation.gov.uk/

Legislation with particular relevance to the construction industry include:

- Construction Design and Management Regulations 2015 (CDM 2015).
- Management of Health and Safety at Work Regulations 1999.
- Control of Asbestos Regulations 2006.
- Health and Safety (Consultation with Employees) Regulations 1996.
- Reporting of Injuries, Diseases and Dangerous Occurrences Regulations 2013 (RIDDOR).
- Work at Height Regulations 2007 (Amended).
- Lifting Operations and Lifting Equipment Regulations 1998 (LOLER).
- Provisions and Use of Work Equipment 1998 (PUWER).

To help interpret the legislation HSE publish Approved Codes of Practice (ACoPs) and Guidance which can be obtained via Construction Industry Publications Ltd. Telephone: 0870 078 4400 Fax: 0870 078 4401 Email: sales@cip-books.com Website: www.cip-books.com or the HSE Bookshop https://books.hse.gov.uk.

13.2   HSE Contact

HSE does not answer general health and safety questions. If you need to engage the services of a health and safety consultant, you may wish to visit the Occupational Safety and Health Consultants Register (OSHCR).

How to get more Information and Help

However;

- If you have a specific question on how the health and safety law applies to a particular issue at your workplace, for which HSE is the enforcing authority and you cannot find the answer on their website, then you can ask HSE by completing the online advice form . HSE aim to respond within 30 working days.

- If you are an employee or a member of the public and you think the health and safety law is being broken, or minimum standards are being ignored within the workplace you can also raise your concern with HSE.

If you are unable to complete the online advice form yourself, you can phone 0300 003 1747 during office hours - 8.30 am to 5.00 pm, Monday to Friday, Wednesday 10.00 am to 5.00 pm, and a call handler will complete the form for you.

13.3   Guidance on CDM

Guidance on CDM 2015 for all the dutyholders is available on a free download at:

CITB ConstructionSkills – www.citb-constructionskills.co.uk

13.4   Health and Safety Management

The following documents are amongst those available from Construction Industry Publications Ltd: www.cip-books.com

- Health and Safety at Law Poster (mandatory).
- Construction Health and Safety Manual.
- Report Books for Work at Height, PUWER, LOLER, PPE, Training and Induction.
- Risk Guide and Risk Pad.
- Induction DVD.

Occupational Health Guidance information can be accessed via the industry scheme Constructing Better Health – www.cbhscheme.com/